Access Your Online Resources

Demystifying Executive Functioning is accompanied by a number of printable online materials, designed to ensure that this resource best supports your professional needs.

Go to https://resourcecentre.routledge.com/speechmark and click on the cover of this book.

Answer the question prompt using your copy of the book to gain access to the online content.

DEMYSTIFYING EXECUTIVE FUNCTIONING

Have you ever taught a learner who either doesn't start their work or starts but never finishes? A learner who produces some brilliant but unrelated work? A learner who can't seem to remember your instructions?

Often, these are the learners who, despite a thirst for learning, lack the skills required for classroom success due to a potential unmet need linked to executive functioning. This accessible guide explores the executive functioning difficulties that learners may face which can pose as barriers to learning in the classroom and lead to mislabelling as 'naughty', 'lazy' or 'inattentive'. The chapters:

- address key topics including working memory, organisation, self-monitoring and impulse control;

- contain a practical toolkit of resources, including helpful sheets to share with staff, parents and carers;

- demystify the science and theory behind executive functioning;

- provide practical advice, tried-and-tested strategies and 'what to do' solutions; and

- place a focus throughout on meeting needs in the classroom through adaptive, well-scaffolded and high-quality teaching.

With hands-on, simple and impactful advice, this guide will enable the reader to put all they have learned about executive functioning into practice to best support the learners in their care. It will be key reading for special educational needs (SEN) coordinators, as well as practising classroom teachers and early careers teachers.

Beccie Hawes is currently the CEO of Cadmus Inclusive, a SEN advisory support service. She is the author of five other SEN-themed books and writes extensively in this area. She has also developed educational resources to support learners with additional needs. Beccie is passionate about celebrating learning differences and strives to support schools to think differently to ensure that every learner has the chance to shine. She is a mum/stepmum to four fantastic young men and Harry and Lola, her family's dogs.

DEMYSTIFYING EXECUTIVE FUNCTIONING

A PRACTICAL CLASSROOM GUIDE AND TOOLKIT

Beccie Hawes

Routledge
Taylor & Francis Group

LONDON AND NEW YORK

Designed cover image: Getty Images

First published 2026
by Routledge
4 Park Square, Milton Park, Abingdon, Oxon OX14 4RN

and by Routledge
605 Third Avenue, New York, NY 10158

Routledge is an imprint of the Taylor & Francis Group, an informa business

British Library Cataloguing-in-Publication Data
A catalogue record for this book is available from the British Library

ISBN: 9781032877198 (hbk)
ISBN: 9781032877136 (pbk)
ISBN: 9781003534075 (ebk)

DOI: 10.4324/9781003534075

Typeset in DIN Pro
by Deanta Global Publishing Services, Chennai, India

Access the Support Material: https://resourcecentre.routledge.com/speechmark

For my tribe.
Your vibe attracts your tribe and I'm so grateful and glad that my vibe has brought me my wonderful tribe of my Hawes family of 'good lads', my Cadmus Inclusive family of beautiful battle unicorns and my doggo family Harry and Lola – the very bestest of all the boys and goodest of all the girls.

A special shoutout goes to my husband, Tony, and my partner in crime, Emma.
Tony – always was and always will be.
Emma – keep on the journey. Our tiny humans need you!

A cheeky bonus mention for my Uncle Brian - for being unapologetically you, always honest, loving us all unconditionally and keeping me grounded in the values of being a Shields. Thank you!

Finally, for every single tiny, medium-sized and large human that I have ever worked with – you are all incredible. Never let anyone dull your sparkle!

CONTENTS

Contents

Chapter 1
WHAT IS EXECUTIVE FUNCTIONING?

Introduction

In any classroom or learning environment, regardless of the age or stage of our learners, we are constantly asking them to do 'stuff'. This 'stuff' could be anything from following a short, simple instruction to preparing and delivering a presentation about previous learning, completing a science investigation or reading a passage from the beginning to the end and answering questions about it. To succeed at any classroom task, we need our learners not only to have and demonstrate the specific subject/topic knowledge and understanding, but also to have the project management skills to complete the tasks that we set from the planning stage through to completion. To succeed, our learners need to be able to:

- recall previous learning while holding and processing new information to give an output;
- self-monitor;
- plan and prioritise;
- initiate the task;
- organise themselves and the required resources;
- control their impulses;
- control their emotions; and
- think flexibly.

This all needs to happen automatically, often simultaneously and against the backdrop of a busy learning environment full of other learners. These are the essential lifelong learning skills that we don't necessarily explicitly teach. They develop through osmosis as we expose our learners to a variety of classroom experiences. We refer to this set of skills as 'executive function' – more on this later!

DOI: 10.4324/9781003534075-1

Please allow me to introduce a learner who, for many of you, will sound familiar. I would like you to meet Joe. Joe could be in any year group. Here is a flavour of Joe collected in his learning profile.

Joe is a learner who is potentially at risk of many things, such as:

- being identified as non-compliant and difficult because of his failure to follow instructions;
- being judged to be lazy because he does not start or complete schoolwork;
- being described as oversensitive and overly emotional as he becomes dysregulated quickly;
- developing friendship difficulties within his peer group;
- being branded as disruptive in lessons;
- being known as disorganised;
- underachieving due to not being able to access learning tasks independently;
- falling out of love with learning;
- becoming frequently emotionally dysregulated;
- being identified as having special educational needs; and
- accumulating a number of consequences as staff take a behavioural approach to managing him in the classroom, potentially leading to suspension or exclusion.

There is a lot to unpick here and, as busy teachers, it could be easy to become frustrated by the many unmet needs that Joe appears to be communicating through his behaviours in the classroom.

[Reflection points in a shaded, curved-edge box]

REFLECTION POINT

- Can you think of a learner who experiences similar difficulties to Joe?
- How do their needs present themselves in your learning environment?

I'm going to 'park' Joe for the moment; but I want you to keep him in mind while we consider what executive functioning actually is.

What is executive functioning?

'Executive functioning' is an overarching term that describes a suite of cognitive processes and mental skills that support us in planning, monitoring and successfully executing our goals, even when interrupted or distracted. Our executive function skills are processed in the prefrontal cortex of the brain – the part of the brain that resides directly behind the

TABLE 1.1 Learning profile

Learner profile	
Strengths, gifts, talents and interests	• Joe is a creative learner – he is fantastic at drawing, problem solving and construction-based tasks. • He can be very articulate and has a lovely sense of humour. • Joe enjoys online gaming and spending time outside with his friends – particularly bike riding.
Attention and listening skills	• Joe can show appropriate levels of interest in highly personally motivating tasks, provided that he is actively involved in 'doing'. • Joe's attention can wander. He will easily lose the thread of what he is doing and start something else which is often unrelated to the task in progress. Levels of task abandonment are high. His workbooks contain many incomplete pieces of work. • Joe needs to be reminded to listen carefully. He responds better to having one instruction at a time to complete. • He often appears to have completely forgotten what has been said to him.
Organisation skills	• Joe constantly loses things. He can travel from his own classroom to the classroom next door and lose all his equipment on the way. He often can't explain where it has gone or what has happened. • On a good day and with adult reminders, Joe does respond well to a visual task timeline or a checklist to aid his organisation. • Joe finds it difficult to manage his time. He is often late for lessons.
Task initiation, maintenance and completion skills	• This varies on a day-to-day basis. Joe will sometimes need direct adult intervention to begin a task or support to keep going and finish it. • Many tasks are begun and not completed or, halfway through, turn into something unrelated to what he should have produced. • On good days, Joe's work can be coherent and shows a super understanding and application of lesson content and his knowledge and understanding; but this is very inconsistent. • He works much more effectively with one-to-one adult support to keep him focused. Without this, very little is achieved. • When Joe does begin a task, he often does not plan what he needs to do. He 'dives in' impulsively, which means that his work is not always well thought through. • He will often start tasks without gathering any of the resources that he needs.
Recall	• Joe can remember knowledge-based facts from lessons but finds recalling instructions difficult. • Tasks requiring Joe to 'hold' and process information or tasks with several small steps and information to instantly recall and use pose significant challenges. Often, adults need to help him to make jottings to recall steps within a task; otherwise, he loses his place and gives up.
Social skills	• Joe makes friends easily. He is popular among his peers. • At times, Joe can become dysregulated very quickly in games where there are lots of rules to follow or where he needs to adopt a specific role. This can lead to arguments. • His peers complain that he does not always listen to them so can misinterpret situations.

(Continued)

TABLE 1.1 (Continued)

Learner profile	
Understanding and use of language	• Joe is a very articulate learner with an extensive vocabulary which he deploys well. • He can find recounting an event difficult as he experiences difficulties with sequencing information. This can result in muddles. • Joe understands subject-specific vocabulary and can follow instructions (provided that he is focused).
Classroom behaviour	• Joe often calls out his immediate needs, wants and answers to questions. • He can easily become upset and communicates this through very emotional outbursts. These can take the form of slamming his pencil on the table or kicking the table legs. He will often get up and walk out of the classroom. • On occasion, Joe can appear to be refusing to complete tasks and follow instructions. • Often, Joe can appear to be set in his ways. Once he has made his mind up, it is difficult to change it. He can be very stubborn. • Joe can often be off task and can distract others. This then leads to him receiving consequences. His behaviour record shows that he is accumulating many consequences. Senior leaders are monitoring this closely. • Generally, Joe is the cause of a lot of low-level disruptive behaviour. This is not conducive to a positive learning environment for him and his peers. • Joe has to be frequently reminded not to fidget, tap his pencil repetitively, make silly noises or swing on his chair.
Attainment overview	• Joe does not appear to be meeting his potential. • He is performing at age-related expectations for PE, design technology, personal, social and health education and performing arts; but it appears that as the workload in these subjects increases, his progress is slowing. • In English, maths, science, humanities and computing, Joe is working below age-related expectations.

forehead. Other parts of the brain that are closely connected to the prefrontal cortex are also involved.

We can break down executive functioning skills into the following areas:

- working memory – a temporary store that holds a limited amount of information for immediate use;
- self-monitoring – in the classroom, this is the ability to self-assess and identify feelings, needs, wants, successes and when things are not working out as we would hope;
- planning and prioritising – deciding how we will go about a task and in what order;
- task initiation – the ability to begin a task;
- organisation – the ability to organise our physical and mental environment, such as the resources that we need for a task and how we will work through the stages involved;

- impulse control – the ability to stop, think and plan before we begin a task and to maintain our focus;
- emotional control – the capacity to manage our emotions and feelings to respond appropriately to them; and
- flexible thinking – the ability to think in different ways when completing a task and to switch between tasks.

These skills are essential for any learner to be able to access learning in a busy classroom, but they are not necessarily skills that we explicitly teach. They also help us to make positive choices about how we communicate our needs through our behaviour and allow us to make healthy choices not only for ourselves, but for our families too. We will look at each one of these areas in detail later.

When considering executive functioning, it is important to note that our learners are not born with these skills in place but do have the potential to develop them. However, as with anything that we learn, some learners need more support than others to develop executive functioning skills. The development of executive functioning skills can be made more challenging or inhibited for learners who have not had their basic human needs met. For example, perhaps they have spent time in adverse environments in which they have experienced neglect and/or abuse or have been exposed to traumatic events. This can disturb the architecture of the developing brain, resulting in the impairment of the development of executive function.

To put this into context, let us consider what might for you be some familiar situations:

- cooking dinner for your family while refereeing a disagreement between two of your children and answering the telephone at the same time;
- remembering directions given to you by a passer-by when your satnav has let you down; and
- counting to ten and taking a deep breath when the car in front suddenly turns left without indicating, instead of sounding your car horn (or worse).

In all these situations, our executive functioning skills support us in planning what we need to do and in what order, remembering and processing information, focusing our attention on the right thing at the right time, helping us to manage our impulses, switching quickly between tasks and juggling multiple tasks. Our executive functioning could be compared to the head chef of a top restaurant who must ensure that their team brings all the elements of a meal together on the plate at the restaurant pass at precisely the same time to delight their diners.

It could be argued that acquiring the essential early building blocks of these indispensable skills for adult life is perhaps one of the most important and challenging tasks of a learner's time in early years education. Their strength is critical to learning and healthy development throughout childhood, adolescence and beyond.

At this point, it is worth considering what the difference between executive functioning and metacognition is and how they complement each other. At its most straightforward level, 'metacognition' can be described as thinking about thinking. It is often defined as the awareness and understanding of our own thought processes. Our metacognitive thinking allows us to be aware of our own learning and memory and make conscious choices about how we approach and learn. If we can use our metacognitive skills well when learning, we can recognise when something is going well and do more of it but also recognise when we are finding a task challenging and adjust our approach accordingly. This means that we can become self-regulated learners.

The relationship between executive functioning and metacognition is a dynamic one. They operate in isolation, but their processes are interrelated. A classroom example of this is reading comprehension. To establish meaning when reading, the reader must continuously monitor their understanding of the text while decoding each word. They need to realise when meaning is lost and then apply a strategy to rectify the situation, such as re-reading a sentence that was not fully processed or looking up the definition of a word that they did not understand. This is metacognition in action. Our executive functioning skills support this metacognitive approach in many ways. One example of this is by utilising flexible thinking. Let's say that you have just read the phrase, 'We came to a fork in the road.' Two meanings may spring to mind here. Did you find an actual piece of cutlery lying in the middle of the road; or did you come to a junction where one road becomes two divergent roads? We need to think flexibly to decide which one makes the most sense in the context of the text.

EXECUTIVE FUNCTIONING IN A NUTSHELL

Executive functioning is a group of cognitive processes and mental skills that support us to plan, monitor and successfully execute a goal. These skills include:

- working memory;
- self-monitoring;
- planning and prioritising;
- task initiation;
- organisation;
- impulse control;
- emotional control; and
- flexible thinking.

What can executive functioning difficulties look like in the classroom?

The following quotes are from learners whom I have spoken with about their executive functioning difficulties. The first comes from a Year 7 learner who, I think, describes their difficulties with executive functioning in the classroom very eloquently:

> Imagine how it feels when every time the teacher tells you to do something you are not sure how long it will take you, what the steps involved are and how you will get to the finished point that they want. Imagine having to work hard to remember everything and to link up the learning and stay focused. I just get into a muddle and then I get into trouble. It's not that I won't do the work that the teacher wants me to do; it's just that I get into a mess when I try to do it. This makes me frustrated and then I get angry.

The second comes from a Year 1 learner, who told me:

> I don't like it when I don't have my visual timeline. I don't know what to do and I do the wrong things. This makes me worried. When I am worried, I do wriggling and I forget stuff. Then the teacher gets sad because I have done none of the work.

Now, let's return to Joe – our 'at-risk' learner – and explore his classroom experience.

Considering what we now know about executive functioning, and from a professionally curious standpoint: could it be possible that Joe experiences some kind of executive functioning differences in comparison to his peers? Let's look at it like this.

TABLE 1.2 Joe's executive functioning

Executive functioning skill	From Joe's learner profile
Working memory	• Joe needs to be reminded to listen carefully. He responds better to being given one instruction at a time to complete. • He often appears to have completely forgotten what has been said to him. • Joe can remember knowledge-based facts from lessons but finds recalling instructions difficult. • Task requiring Joe to 'hold' and process information or tasks with several small steps and information to instantly recall and use pose significant challenges. Often, adults need to help him to make jottings to recall steps within a task; otherwise, he loses his place and gives up. • He can find recounting an event difficult as he experiences difficulties with sequencing information. This can result in muddles. • Joe often calls out his immediate needs, wants and answers to questions.
Self-monitoring	• Joe's attention can wander. He will easily lose the thread of what he is doing and start something else which is often unrelated to the task in progress. Levels of task abandonment are high. His workbooks contain many incomplete pieces of work. • Joe has to be frequently reminded not to fidget, tap his pencil repetitively, make silly noises or swing on his chair.
Planning and prioritising	• When Joe does begin a task, he often does not plan what he needs to do. He 'dives in' impulsively, which means that his work is not always well thought through. • He will often start tasks without gathering any of the resources that he needs.
Task initiation	• This varies on a day-to-day basis. Joe will sometimes need direct adult intervention to begin a task or support to keep going and finish. • Many tasks are begun and not completed or, halfway through, turn into something unrelated to what he should have produced. • On good days, his work can be coherent and shows a super understanding and application of lesson content and his knowledge and understanding; but this is very inconsistent. • He works much more effectively with one-to-one adult support to keep him focused. Without this, very little is achieved.
Organisation	• Joe constantly loses things. He can travel from his own classroom to the classroom next door and lose all his equipment on the way. He often can't explain where it has gone or what has happened. • On a good day and with adult reminders, he does respond well to a visual task timeline or a checklist to aid his organisation. • Joe finds it difficult to manage his time. He is often late for lessons.
Impulse control	• Joe often calls out his immediate needs, wants and answers to questions. • He can often be off task and can distract others. This then leads to him receiving consequences. His behaviour record shows that he is accumulating many consequences. Senior leaders are monitoring this closely. • Generally, he is the cause of a lot of low-level disruptive behaviour which is not conducive to a positive learning environment for him and his peers.

(Continued)

TABLE 1.2 (Continued)

Executive functioning skill	From Joe's learner profile
Emotional control	• At times, Joe can become dysregulated very quickly in games where there are lots of rules to follow or where he needs to adopt a specific role. This can lead to arguments.
Flexible thinking	• On occasion, Joe can appear to be refusing to complete tasks and follow instructions. • Often, Joe can appear to be set in his ways. Once he has made his mind up, it is difficult to change it. He can be very stubborn.

REFLECTION POINT

• Does looking at Joe's challenges through a different lens change your perception of him?

When we look at Joe's classroom presentation against the distinct areas of executive functioning, we can see that it is well worth examining how Joe's behaviour presents through a different lens. I would argue that it is perfectly possible that his 'behaviour' is a method of communicating his frustration at being unable to show what he knows as he struggles to execute the 'stuff' that we are asking him to do. His learning profile states that: 'On good days his work can be coherent and shows a super understanding and application of lesson content and his knowledge and understanding; but this is very inconsistent.'

To test this hypothesis, rather than persisting with a behaviour management approach of reprimands and sanctions, perhaps we should be looking at what we can offer as part of a high-quality adaptive teaching approach to scaffold his executive functioning skills. Joe may be experiencing a case of 'can't' as opposed to 'won't'.

To provide effective support for learners such as Joe, the first thing that we need to do is to identify who may have a potential executive functioning-related need. The identification tool presented in Table 3 can be used to identify a potential executive functioning-related difficulty and can help to focus on which areas to prioritise for support.

How to use the identification tool

The tool can be used flexibly: for some learners, you might wish to focus on one area of executive functioning as a starting point; while for others, you might consider all of the areas.

For each area, consider how often you see the statements in the 'What you might see' section and record the frequency. This need not be exact. For those statements that are occurring the most frequently, you can then look in the 'Toolkit signposts' column on the right-hand side of the table. This provides you with a signpost to a tool from this book and where to find it as a form of quick reference.

TABLE 1.3 Identification tool

Area of executive functioning	What you might see	Frequency			Toolkit signposts
Working memory		**Most lessons/ activities**	**50–75% of lessons/ activities**	**Rarely**	
	Has difficulties with following instructions.				**Working memory tools:** 3, 4, 5, 6, 9, 10, 12 and 14 **Planning and prioritising tools:** 1 and 3 **Task initiation tools:** 3 **Organisation tools:** 11 **Emotional control tools:** 6
	When information is presented, appears to become 'overloaded' quickly.				**Working memory tools:** 1, 2, 4, 5, 7, 8, 9, 10, 12 and 14 **Self-monitoring tools:** 11 and 13 **Task initiation tools:** 12 **Emotional control tools** 6
	Has difficulties with 'holding' information in mind and using it to provide an outcome/answer.				**Working memory tools:** 4, 6, 8, 9, 10, 12, 13 and 14 **Planning and prioritising tools:** 1 and 3 **Task initiation tools:** 3
	Experiences high levels of task abandonment.				**Working memory tools:** 1, 4, 6, 9, 10 and 12 **Planning and prioritising tools:** 1 and 3
	Frequently needs to restart tasks.				**Working memory tools:** 1, 4, 6, 9, 10 and 12
	Has difficulties with place keeping within a task.				**Working memory tools:** 1, 2, 6 and 9 **Planning and prioritising tools:** 1 and 3
	Appears to 'miss' task details.				**Working memory tools:** 4, 5, 6, 7, 9, 10 and 12 **Planning and prioritising tools:** 1, 3 and 10

(Continued)

TABLE 1.3 (Continued)

Area of executive functioning	What you might see	Frequency			Toolkit signposts
		Most lessons/ activities	**50–75% of lessons/ activities**	**Rarely**	
Working memory					
	Calls out and/ or interrupts – needs to share information/ answers immediately.				**Working memory tools:** 4, 6, 9, 11, 13 and 14 **Impulse control tools:** 5 and 8
	Finds solving problems with more than one step challenging.				**Working memory tools:** 1, 4, 6, 9, 10 and 12 **Self-monitoring tools:** 11 **Planning and prioritising tools:** 1 and 3
	Can be easily distracted.				**Working memory tools:** 1, 4, 6 and 9
	Has difficulties with organising themselves and the resources required for learning.				**Working memory tools:** 6 and 9 **Planning and prioritising tools:** 6 and 7 **Task initiation tools:** 1 **Organisation tools:** 2, 5, 6, 7 and 10
	Appears to be forgetful.				**Working memory tools:** 1, 2, 3, 7, 9, 10, 11, 12, 13 and 14
	Forgets what they have been asked to do.				**Working memory tools:** 1, 2, 3, 7, 9, 10, 11, 12, 13 and 14 **Planning and prioritising tools:** 1 and 3 **Task initiation tools:** 3 and 6 **Organisation tools:** 11

(Continued)

TABLE 1.3 (Continued)

Area of executive functioning	What you might see	Frequency			Toolkit signposts
Self-monitoring		**Most lessons/ activities**	**50–75% of lessons/ activities**	**Rarely**	
	Has difficulties with identifying their own feelings.				**Self-monitoring tools:** 1, 3, 6 and 11
	When completing a task, has difficulties with identifying what is working well.				**Self-monitoring tools:** 4, 7 and 9 **Planning and prioritising tools:** 11 and 13 **Organisation tools:** 1 **Emotional control tools:** 7
	When completing a task, has difficulties with identifying what is not working well.				**Self-monitoring tools:** 14, 7 and 9 **Planning and prioritising tools:** 11 and 13 **Emotional control tools:** 7
	Will continue with a task in the same way even if they are not succeeding.				**Self-monitoring tools:** 2, 4 and 7 **Planning and prioritising tools:** 5
	Inaccurately self-assesses strengths and areas to develop.				**Self-monitoring tools:** 4, 9, 12, 13 and 14
	Has difficulties with spotting errors in own work.				**Self-monitoring tools:** 7, 9, 14 and 16
	Appears to be copying or checking their own actions against what their peers are doing.				**Self-monitoring tools:** 9 and 10 **Planning and prioritising tools:** 9
	Can appear reluctant to seek support from others.				**Self-monitoring tools:** 5 and 13
	Does not use provided scaffolding resources.				**Self-monitoring tools:** 8 and 9

(Continued)

TABLE 1.3 (Continued)

Area of executive functioning	What you might see	Frequency			Toolkit signposts
Self-monitoring		Most lessons/ activities	50–75% of lessons/ activities	Rarely	
	Does not check their own work.				**Self-monitoring tools:** 5, 7, 9 and 16
	Has difficulties with noticing and then responding to social cues from peers.				**Self-monitoring tools:** 10 **Emotional control tools:** 9 and 10
	Demonstrates sensory seeking/ sensory avoiding behaviours which may support self-regulation.				**Monitoring tools:** 15 **Planning and prioritising tools:** 13 **Emotional control tools:** 2 and 10

Area of executive functioning	What you might see	Frequency			Toolkit signposts
Planning and prioritising		Most lessons/ activities	50–75% of lessons/ activities	Rarely	
	Finds it challenging to think ahead.				**Planning and prioritising tools:** 1, 2, 3, 8, 12 and 13 **Working memory tools:** 12 **Self-monitoring tools:** 2, 7, 9 and 11
	Can often see the end result but cannot identify the steps required to get to this.				**Planning and prioritising tools:** 1, 3, 5, 8, 9, 12 and 13 **Working memory tools:** 12 **Self-monitoring tools:** 2, 7, 9 and 11
	Appears to be disorganised.				**Planning and prioritising tools:** 4, 6, 7 and 10 **Self-monitoring tools:** 7

(Continued)

TABLE 1.3 (Continued)

Area of executive functioning	What you might see	Frequency			Toolkit signposts
Planning and prioritising		**Most lessons/ activities**	**50–75% of lessons/ activities**	**Rarely**	
	Appears to be impulsive.				**Planning and prioritising tools:** 2, 3, 4, 8 and 12 **Working memory tools:** 12 **Self-monitoring tools:** 4, 9 and 11
	Does not consider the future consequences of their immediate actions.				**Planning and prioritising tools:** 2, 5, 8, 11, 12 and 13 **Self-monitoring tools:** 4 and 9
	Does not have the correct resources for a task.				**Planning and prioritising tools:** 6 **Organisation tools:** 2, 7 and 10
	Appears to always be in the 'here and now'.				**Planning and prioritising tools:** 1, 2, 3, 4, 8, 11, 12 and 13 **Self-monitoring tools:** 4, 7, 9 and 11

Area of executive functioning	What you might see	Frequency			Toolkit signposts
Task initiation		**Most lessons/ activities**	**50–75% of lessons/ activities**	**Rarely**	
	Has difficulties with starting tasks independently.				**Task initiation tools:** 1, 2, 3, 5, 6, 7 and 8 **Working memory tools:** 1, 4, 8 and 12 **Self-monitoring tools:** 1, 4 and 11 **Planning and prioritising tools:** 1, 3, 6 and 9
	Displays work avoidance behaviours.				**Task initiation tools:** 1, 2, 3, 5, 7 and 8 **Working memory tools:** 1, 4, 8 and 12 **Self-monitoring tools:** 4 and 11 **Planning and prioritising tools:** 1, 6 and 9

(Continued)

TABLE 1.3 (Continued)

Area of executive functioning	What you might see	Frequency			Toolkit signposts
Task initiation		**Most lessons/ activities**	**50–75% of lessons/ activities**	**Rarely**	
	Has difficulties with initiating conversations.				**Task initiation tools:** 2 and 4 **Emotional control tools:** 9 and 10
	Is happy for others to take the lead.				**Task initiation tools:** 2 and 4 **Flexible thinking tools:** 7
	Can appear to be unfocused.				**Task initiation tools:** 1, 5, 6, 8 and 9 **Working memory tools:** 4, 12 and 13 **Self-monitoring tools:** 6, 9 and 15 **Planning and prioritising tools:** 4, 12 and 13
	Starts a task independently but takes a long time to do so.				**Task initiation tools:** 1, 2, 3, 5, 6, 7 and 8 **Working memory tools:** 1, 4, 8 and 12 **Self-monitoring tools:** 1, 4 and 11 **Planning and prioritising tools:** 1, 3, 6 and 9
	Spends a long time observing what others are doing before beginning a task.				**Task initiation tools:** 3, 5, 7 and 8 **Self-monitoring tools:** 12 **Planning and prioritising tools:** 9
	Seeks immediate support before trialling independently.				**Task initiation tools:** 3, 6, 7, 8 and 9 **Working memory tools:** 9 **Self-monitoring tools:** 1 **Planning and prioritising tools:** 9

(Continued)

TABLE 1.3 (Continued)

Area of executive functioning	What you might see	Frequency			Toolkit signposts
Organisation		Most lessons/ activities	50–75% of lessons/ activities	Rarely	
	Has difficulties with time management.				**Organisation tools:** 1, 4 and 12 **Planning and prioritising tools:** 1 and 7
	Appears to be forgetful of things such as PE kit, homework and specific lesson resources.				**Organisation tools:** 4 **Working memory tools:** 1, 2, 3, 7, 9, 10, 11, 12, 13 and 14 **Task initiation tools:** 3
	Finds it difficult to select the right resources for a task.				**Organisation tools:** 2, 3, 4 and 7 **Planning and prioritising tools:** 1 and 7
	Gets lost in tasks easily so work produced is often muddled.				**Organisation tools:** 8 and 12 **Working memory tools:** 12 **Planning and prioritising tools:** 1
	Misses deadlines.				**Organisation tools:** 3, 1 and 12 **Planning and prioritising tools:** 2 and 4
	Often leaves things until the last minute.				**Organisation tools:** 1, 3 and 4 **Planning and prioritising tools:** 2 and 4 **Task initiation tools:** 5 and 7
	Is untidy.				**Organisation tools:** 2, 5, 7 and 10 **Planning and prioritising tools:** 7
	Loses things easily.				**Organisation tools:** 2, 5, 6 and 10

(Continued)

TABLE 1.3 (Continued)

Area of executive functioning	What you might see	Frequency			Toolkit signposts
Organisation		**Most lessons/ activities**	**50–75% of lessons/ activities**	**Rarely**	
	Has difficulties with sequencing.				**Organisation tools:** 8, 9, 11 and 12 **Working memory tools:** 3 **Self-monitoring tools:** 13 **Planning and prioritising tools:** 3 and 7 **Task initiation tools:** 6
	Finds it challenging to follow a sequence of steps in a task or the stages in multi-step instructions.				**Organisation tools:** 8, 9, 11 and 12 **Working memory tools:** 3 and 9 **Self-monitoring tools:** 13 **Planning and prioritising tools:** 3 and 7 **Task initiation tools:** 3 and 6
	Gets muddled easily.				**Organisation tools:** 8, 9, 11 and 12 **Working memory tools:** 1, 3, 4 and 7 **Self-monitoring tools:** 13 **Planning and prioritising tools:** 1, 3, 7 and 10

Area of executive functioning	What you might see	Frequency			Toolkit signposts
Impulse control		**Most lessons/ activities**	**50–75% of lessons/ activities**	**Rarely**	
	'Dives in' to tasks and situations, appearing not to think before acting.				**Impulse control tools:** 1, 2, 3, 8 and 11 **Working memory tools:** 1 and 2 **Self-monitoring tools:** 7 **Planning and prioritising tools:** 1, 3 and 8

(Continued)

TABLE 1.3 (Continued)

Area of executive functioning	What you might see	Frequency			Toolkit signposts
		Most lessons/ activities	50–75% of lessons/ activities	Rarely	
Impulse control					
	Does not link consequences to actions.				**Impulse control tools:** 1, 2, 3, 9 and 10 **Self-monitoring tools:** 10 **Planning and prioritising tools:** 1 and 3
	Is easily distracted.				**Impulse control tools:** 11 **Working memory tools:** 4
	Distracts others.				**Impulse control tools:** 5, 8 and 11 **Working memory tools:** 4
	Has difficulties with following instructions.				**Impulse control tools:** 4 and 11 **Working memory tools:** 5 and 12 **Planning and prioritising tools:** 3 **Organisation tools:** 11 **Task initiation tools:** 3
	Appears to not think of others before acting.				**Impulse control tools:** 1, 2, 3 and 10
	Calls out answers.				**Impulse control tools:** 5 and 8
	Has difficulties with turn taking.				**Impulse control tools:** 6, 7 and 9 **Planning and prioritising tools:** 4
	Finds it hard to wait.				**Impulse control tools:** 4, 5, 7 and 8
	Shares information, needs and/ or wants immediately.				**Impulse control tools:** 4 and 5

(Continued)

TABLE 1.3 (Continued)

Area of executive functioning	What you might see	Frequency			Toolkit signposts
Impulse control		**Most lessons/ activities**	**50–75% of lessons/ activities**	**Rarely**	
	Finds it challenging to follow rules in games/shared tasks with peers.				**Impulse control tools:** 6, 7, 8 and 9
	Has difficulties with seeing a task through to the end.				**Impulse control tools:** 7 **Self-monitoring tools:** 7 **Planning and prioritising tools:** 13
	Has difficulties with sharing.				**Impulse control tools:** 6, 7 and 10
	Experiences quick changes in emotions.				**Impulse control tools:** 8, 9 and 10 **Working memory tools:** 13 **Self-monitoring tools:** 1, 6 and 15 **Planning and prioritising tools:** 5 **Emotional control tools:** 1, 10, 12 and 13
	Focuses on the end goal/outcome.				**Impulse control tools:** 1, 2, 3, 5, 7 and 9 **Planning and prioritising tools:** 1, 3 and 8
	Can seek instant gratification.				**Impulse control tools:** 5, 7 and 11 **Planning and prioritising tools:** 1 and 2

(Continued)

TABLE 1.3 (Continued)

Area of executive functioning	What you might see	Frequency			Toolkit signposts
Emotional control		**Most lessons/ activities**	**50–75% of lessons/ activities**	**Rarely**	
	Finds it hard to identify their own emotions.				**Emotional control tools:** 1, 2, 12 and 13
	Emotions can change very quickly.				**Emotional control tools:** 2, 5, 7, 9, 10, 11 and 12
	Becomes frustrated easily.				**Emotional control tools:** 12, 3, 5, 7 and 11 **Planning and prioritising tools:** 1 and 3
	Can appear to become overwhelmed.				**Emotional control tools:** 2, 4, 5, 6, 7, 8, 9 and 10 **Working memory tools:** 2, 3 and 4 **Self-monitoring tools:** 2, 4 and 11 **Task initiation tools:** 3 and 6 **Organisation tools:** 1 and 11
	Reactions can appear to be disproportionate to the situation.				**Emotional control tools:** 1, 2, 10, 12 and 13
	Withdraws from situations that they perceive to be difficult.				**Emotional control tools:** 2, 4, 5 and 10
	Has difficulties with anger management.				**Emotional control tools:** 1, 2, 5, 9 and 10
	Can be involved in arguments with peers.				**Emotional control tools:** 12, 11 and 13 **Impulse control tools:** 6, 7 and 10
	Can be perceived by others to be argumentative.				**Emotional control tools:** 1, 11 and 13 **Impulse control tools:** 6, 7 and 10
	Can be perceived by others to be defiant.				**Emotional control tools:** 2, 4, 11 and 13 **Impulse control tools:** 9 and 10

(*Continued*)

TABLE 1.3 (Continued)

Area of executive functioning	What you might see	Frequency			Toolkit signposts
Flexible thinking		**Most lessons/ activities**	**50–75% of lessons/ activities**	**Rarely**	
	Has only one approach to a task which is used no matter how successful/ unsuccessful.				**Flexible thinking tools:** 1, 2, 4, 6, 8, 9, 11 and 14 **Self-monitoring tools:** 7 and 9 **Planning and prioritising tools:** 11 and 13 **Impulse control tools:** 2 and 3 **Emotional control tools:** 4
	Has difficulties with recognising when an element of a task is completed and that it is time to move on.				**Flexible thinking tools:** 10 **Emotional control tools:** 4
	Needs support to transition from one task to another.				**Flexible thinking tools:** 10 **Task initiation tools:** 6 **Emotional control tools:** 4
	Has difficulties with accepting help from others.				**Flexible thinking tools:** 7 **Self-monitoring tools:** 8
	Does not demonstrate independent problem-solving skills.				**Flexible thinking tools:** 14 **Self-monitoring tools:** 4, 7 and 9 **Planning and prioritising tools:** 11 and 13 **Impulse control tools:** 1, 2 and 3
	Can be perceived by others to be defiant.				**Impulse control tools:** 9 and 10
	Refusals to engage with an activity or follow instructions				**Impulse control tools:** 9 and 10
	Can interpret things in a very literal sense.				**Flexible thinking tools:** 12 and 13

(Continued)

TABLE 1.3 (Continued)

Area of executive functioning	What you might see	Frequency			Toolkit signposts
Flexible thinking		**Most lessons/ activities**	**50–75% of lessons/ activities**	**Rarely**	
	Finds it challenging to accept the viewpoints of others.				**Flexible thinking tools:** 1, 2, 3, 4, 7, 8 and **Self-monitoring tools:** 13 **Planning and prioritising tools:** 11 and 13 **Impulse control tools:** 2 and 3
	Prefers very regular routines.				**Flexible thinking tools:** 5 and 10 **Self-monitoring tools:** 7 and 9 **Impulse control tools:** 7
	Follows routines and processes rigidly.				**Flexible thinking tools:** 1, 2, 4 and 11 **Impulse control tools:** 7

When selecting things from the 'Toolkit signposts' column, you will probably find that there are lots of tools available and that you may wish to try out. It is important not to overwhelm the learner with lots of strategies, resources and tools at once; start small, with one or two things, and do them consistently. Give them time to work and keep reviewing their impact. You can then build from this starting point.

What does a completed identification tool look like?

To give you a flavour of what a completed identification tool looks like, here is a section of one that has been completed for Joe. From the completed 'Working memory' section that follows, we can see that Joe has lots of needs in this area. To make how we will support him more manageable and give us a tighter focus, it makes sense to home in on the statements that seem to apply to 'Most lessons/activities'. Ideally, it would be good to discuss directly with Joe what he is finding the most difficult out of these statements and to ask him to co-design a supportive approach using the signposted resources, strategies and tools in the right-hand column of the identification tool table.

TABLE 1.4 Identification tool completed for Joe

Area of executive functioning	What you might see	Frequency			Signposts to resources, strategies and tools
Working memory		**Most lessons/ activities**	**50–75% of lessons/ activities**	**Rarely**	
	Has difficulties with following instructions.	X			**Working memory tools:** 3, 4, 5, 6, 9, 10, 12 and 14
	When information is presented, appears to become 'overloaded' quickly.	X			**Working memory tools:** 1, 2, 4, 5, 7, 8, 9, 10, 12 and 14
	Has difficulties with 'holding' information in mind and using it to provide an outcome/answer.	X			**Working memory tools:** 4, 6, 8, 9, 10, 12, 13 and 14
	Experiences high levels of task abandonment.	X			**Working memory tools:** 1, 4, 6, 9, 10 and 12
	Frequently needs to restart tasks.	X			**Working memory tools:** 1, 4, 6, 9, 10 and 12
	Has difficulties with place keeping within a task.	X			**Working memory tools:** 1, 2, 6 and 9
	Appears to 'miss' task details.	X			**Working memory tools:** 4, 5, 6, 7, 9, 10 and 12
	Calls out and/or interrupts – needs to share information/ answers immediately.	X			**Working memory tools:** 4, 6, 9, 11, 13 and 14
	Finds solving problems with more than one step challenging.	X			**Working memory tools:** 1, 4, 6, 9, 10 and 12
	Can be easily distracted.	X			**Working memory tools:** 1, 4, 6 and 9
	Has difficulties with organising himself and the resources required for learning.	X			**Working memory tools:** 6 and 9
	Appears to be forgetful.	X			**Working memory tools:** 1, 2, 3, 7, 9, 10, 11, 12, 13 and 14
	Forgets what he has been asked to do.	X			**Working memory tools:** 1, 2, 3, 7, 9, 10, 11, 12, 13 and 14
	Is making less than expected progress.	X			**Working memory tools:** 1, 2, 3, 4, 5, 6, 7, 8, 9, 10, 11, 12, 13 and 14

CHAPTER TAKEAWAYS

- Executive functioning encompasses a group of cognitive processes and mental skills that support us to plan, monitor and successfully execute a goal. These skills include:
  - working memory;
  - self-monitoring;
  - planning and prioritising;
  - task initiation;
  - organisation;
  - impulse control;
  - emotional control; and
  - flexible thinking.
- Learners with executive functioning difficulties can sometimes be misidentified and labelled as difficult. Their behaviours are a means of communicating their struggle to execute the 'stuff' that we are asking them to do as their needs are not identified and met in the classroom.
- Rather than persisting with behaviour management approaches, it is important to explore what we can offer as part of a high-quality adaptive teaching approach to scaffold executive functioning skills.
- To support executive functioning skills effectively, the first thing that we need to do is to identify potential executive functioning-related difficulties and then focus on which areas to prioritise for support.

Chapter 2
WORKING MEMORY

What is it?

In its least complex form, 'memory' can be described as the continuous process of information retention over time. Memory is an essential part of human cognition, since it permits us to recall previous events to aid our understanding and behaviour in the present. Memory also gives us a reference point to support us in making sense of the present and future. Consequently, memory plays a crucial role in learning in the classroom. Under this wider umbrella term of 'memory' sits our working memory.

Imagine that, in the classroom, you had to mentally calculate the answer to 24 x 12. You could do so by splitting the 12 into 10 and 2 to make the multiplication easier to compute:

- 4 x 10 = 240
- 24 x 2 = 48
- 240 + 48 = 288

Which gives you the answer of 288.

> **REFLECTION POINT**
> - How is having a reliable working memory crucial for achieving success with this task?

Having a reliable working memory is crucial to the success of this task. You need it to 'hold' the answer calculated at each step of the task so that you can combine your answers in the last step to arrive at an answer. Your working memory is also needed to help you to keep your place within the task, so that you don't miss out any of the steps or get muddled.

DOI: 10.4324/9781003534075-2

In short, working memory acts as a temporary store that allows us to keep information in mind while we work with it without losing track of the task in hand. Once we have used the information, we forget it because we no longer need it. If we retain it, it just takes up valuable space.

Working memory can be described as being a bit like a Post-it note. We often jot down things that we have to do on a Post-it note as an impermanent reminder. Once the task is done, we put the Post-it note in the bin and the information is gone forever. Learners use working memory in the classroom practically all of the time. They need to retain important information while they work on it in the face of distractions from classmates, wall displays, background noise and their own needs, thoughts and feelings.

Baddeley and Hitch (1974) introduced a model of working memory that suggests it is a multimodal system comprised of three different components: the central executive, the visuospatial sketchpad and the phonological loop. In 2000, this was expanded by Baddeley to include a fourth component: the episodic buffer.

The job of the central executive is, among other things, to direct our attention to relevant information. To this end, it suppresses irrelevant information and actions. It also coordinates our cognitive processes when we complete a task that requires us to do several things at once. It additionally supervises how we link information together and coordinates our other systems that are responsible for the short-term maintenance of information. It controls the

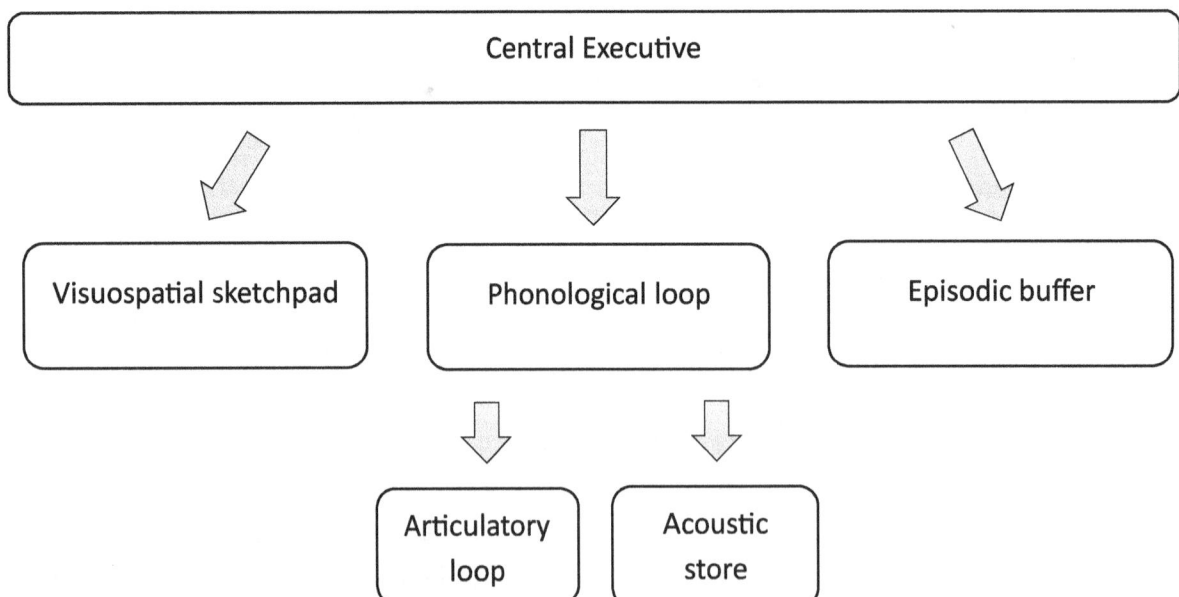

FIGURE 2.1 Model of working memory

flow of information to and from the phonological loop and the visuospatial sketchpad, and processes and manipulates information.

The phonological loop stores phonological information (perhaps more easily thought of as the sound of language). It prevents this sound-based information from being forgotten by continuously refreshing it in a rehearsal loop (the articulatory loop). An example of this is when you continue repeating a security code or telephone number until you can find a paper and pen to record it until needed.

The visuospatial sketchpad is home to visual and spatial information. It can be used, for example, to construct and manipulate visual images and to represent mental maps. An example of this is emembering where you have parked your car or your route home from the supermarket. The sketchpad can be further broken down into a visual subsystem (which deals with shape, colour and texture) and a spatial subsystem (dealing with location).

Finally, the episodic buffer is a limited capacity and temporary storage system that is responsible for integrating information from several places – for example, phonological, visual and spatial information – to create a coherent episode: a memory. It provides the link between working memory and long-term memory.

Our working memory is widely recognised as having limited capacity. There is a personal limit to working memory, with everyone having a relatively fixed capacity that may be greater or less than that of others. Miller (1956) suggested that the capacity limit of information processing in young adults was the 'magical number seven', referring to the seven as 'chunks'. This was regardless of whether those 'chunks' were digits, letters, words or other pieces of information. Later research revealed this number to be dependent on the category of chunks used – for example, approximately seven for digits, six for letters and five for words. It is also dependent on the features of the 'chunks' within a category. For example, attention span is shorter for longer words than for shorter words. Generally, memory span for verbal content such as digits, letters and words depends on the phonological complexity of the content – for example, the number of phonemes or syllables and whether or not the contents are words known to the person. Several other factors can also affect a person's measured span of recall, so it is difficult to identify exactly the capacity of short-term or working memory in terms of a specific number of 'chunks'. However, Cowan (2001) proposes that working memory for young adults has a capacity of about four chunks fewer in children and older adults.

Within the visual domain, it is reported that there is no fixed capacity limit regarding the total number of 'chunks' that can be held in the working memory. Instead, this is proposed as a limited resource that can be flexibly shared between items retained in memory, with some items in the focus of attention being allocated more space and recalled with greater precision (eg, see Bays, Catalao and Husain, 2009).

Working memory and classroom success

In the classroom, learners use their working memory for many routine tasks as well as the business of learning. Many of these tasks place a burden on working memory, as the learner is required to hold some information in mind while engaging in effortful activity. The following non-exhaustive list gives you a flavour of these tasks:

- Copying the date from the board: You need to be able to 'hold' each part that you wish to copy in your visuospatial sketchpad as you look from the board to your page; retrieve what you have seen to write it down; and keep your place so that you do not repeat parts while forming the required letters.
- Recording a sentence that you have composed: You need to be able not only to remember the content of your sentence in the right word order, but also to spell all of the words using a range of encoding strategies, make your handwriting legible, keep the tense consistent and insert the correct punctuation marks.
- Following lengthy, multi-step instructions: You need to remember each instruction in the correct sequence and keep your place within the set of instructions in order to complete the task. This will often be against a time demand.

REFLECTION POINT
- What common tasks can you think of that learners in your classroom have to do daily which place a heavy load on working memory?
- What factors can lead to success and/or failure in these tasks?

Where working memory is concerned, being a successful learner in the classroom can depend in part on working memory capacity. Within the classroom, the differences in working memory capacity between learners of the same age can vary dramatically.

For example, in a typical class of 30 learners aged seven to eight, we could expect at least three of the learners to have the working memory capacity of the average four-year-old child and three others to have the capacity of the average 11-year-old child, which is quite close to adult levels. This can pose a challenge to how we support those who experience working memory difficulties as part of our whole class adaptive teaching approach.

Returning to the model proposed by Baddeley and Hitch (1974), it can be helpful to think of the phonological loop as a limited sound recording device. Some learners can record just seconds and others hours and hours at a time. Similarly, the visuospatial sketchpad can be compared to a television screen. Some learners have a small 32-inch television screen and others have the capacity of a cinema screen. In addition, if we consider that the central executive may become overloaded and send information to the wrong subsystem, it is more understandable as to why the episodic buffer becomes compromised and stores information incorrectly. While we cannot increase working memory capacity, we can offer supportive strategies to ease the burden of recalling and processing simultaneously. More on that later.

Often, learners with working memory difficulties:

- are sociable but may find some strategy-based games where information needs to be held in mind challenging;
- can be more reserved in group activities and avoid direct questions as they are working hard to 'hold onto' information;
- may appear not to be paying attention;
- may abandon tasks;
- lose their place in multi-step tasks or instructions;
- make progress that is not in line with their peers;
- need longer to respond to information and/or instructions;
- can appear to be easily distracted;
- become easily overloaded and therefore overwhelmed and dysregulated; and
- forget the information contained in messages.

To bring all of this to life, the following is a case study of a learner with working memory difficulties.

Working memory in the classroom – a case study

Background information

Sam is working below age-related expectations in most subjects and is making very slow progress in comparison to his peers, despite his best endeavours and lots of intervention comprised of revisiting basic literacy and numeracy catch-up skills. This has been the case throughout his time in school.

Sam is popular with his peers but is a quieter member of the group when working in the classroom. Sam finds schoolwork challenging and feels that he tries harder than his peers to keep up with the work. He feels that school is becoming a frustrating environment.

Recent hearing and vision tests have identified no issues. His family have no concerns regarding his health and wellbeing.

Sam was previously referred to speech and language therapy for assessment. His assessment report identified difficulties with attention and listening skills.

Information from the class teacher

Sam's teacher reports that Sam often fails to keep up with classroom activities. He is described as a well-behaved child but can easily be distracted. His teacher notes that Sam can often fail to listen to instructions and can quickly become frustrated when he gets overloaded with information.

Often, Sam will fail to complete his work. His workbooks are full of half-completed work or work which is disorganised or goes 'off topic'.

Observations

English: writing a recount of a school trip

Sam was asked to copy the date and title of the work from the board:

> Tuesday 18 June
>
> Our Class Visit to the Woods.

Sam quickly lost his place as he copied each word letter by letter. He appeared to work very slowly and deliberately. It appeared that he had started writing the date, got lost in the task and begun writing the title. Sam recorded the following:

> TuesJuOurClasVist

He ran out of time to complete the rest.

Mathematics: using a number line to count on to add two single-digit numbers

Sam was able to identify that the task required him to add 3 and 7 together to arrive at the total.

Sam placed his finger on the number 3 but then found it very challenging to coordinate moving along the number line seven times. He kept counting on and then abandoned the task as he realised he was not sure where to stop.

Computing: developing and inputting a code to move a robot from one location to another

Sam understood the task and could make lots of sensible suggestions regarding the commands needed to move the robot in a sensible and logical direction. He gave each command one at a time. When asked to combine the commands using an 'and' command, Sam ran into difficulty. He missed out commands, resulting in his robot travelling in the wrong direction. He became frustrated and asked to use his timeout card to visit the classroom 'chillout zone'.

Support and impact to date	
Support	**Impact**
Tabletop copy of resources that are to be copied	Greater accuracy in copying but Sam still works slowly – letter by letter.
Task slicing – breaking tasks into smaller stages and issuing them one at a time	This works well as long as a visual timeline is provided.
Basic skills catch-up programme	At times, Sam makes huge leaps forward but then seems to regress. His recall is very variable on a day-to-day basis.
Memory games	Sam gets better at playing the game so recalls more, but this does not seem to transfer as a skill back into his work in the classroom.
Timeout card	Sam uses this well when he becomes overloaded/ overwhelmed and visits the classroom 'chillout zone'. He returns to the group once he has self-regulated.

Next steps

Sam's provision needs reviewing. Although the support implemented to date seems to match well to his needs, we are not seeing the gains we would expect.

REFLECTION POINT

- Do you have learners who experience similar difficulties to Sam?
- What support do you offer to these learners?
- How successful is this support in meeting their needs?

So, how do we support a learner such as Sam? Here are some practical tools. When you look at them, you will see that Sam's school was certainly working in the right direction. With a few refinements and a deeper focus on what he needs to support his working memory, I think that Sam could make lots of progress!

Working memory toolkit

Classroom challenges
• Cognitive overload (becoming overwhelmed when lots of information is presented at once);
• Place keeping;
• Task initiation, maintenance and completion;
• Following instructions;
• Forgetting things – inconsistent recall; and
• Keeping information in mind when completing a task.

Tools

The following tools are all designed to reduce the burden of recall on working memory.

1. When planning lessons, evaluate the working memory demands of learning activities. Activities that pose a big burden include the retention of significant amounts of verbal material with relatively arbitrary content – for example:

   - remembering sequences of numbers or words which are seemingly unrelated;

   - remembering and following lengthy and/or multi-step instructions; and

   - keeping your place in the stages of a multi-step task.

Consider how you can use the following tools to lessen the burden on working memory.

2. Increase the personal meaningfulness or familiarity of lesson content through pre-teaching. We are more likely to recall things that feel familiar. If something feels familiar and is personally motivating, we are more likely to engage with it in a meaningful sense.

3. Use simple language structures and shorter sentences to convey verbal information. Doing this will mean that the learner does not have to 'unpick' what you mean and sequence it again.

4. Reduce concurrent processing demands so that the learner has one thing to do at a time. This reduces the cognitive processing demand.

5. Frequently repeat important information and ask learners to repeat it to each other. Rehearsal really helps.

6. Support information given verbally with a visual and permanent reminder such as:

   - jottings;

   - a checklist;

   - a flowchart;

   - an illustration; or

   - a diagram.

This works effectively as when we learn new information, we store it as an image (think visuospatial sketchpad) or a word (think phonological loop). The word or the image can be used to support the retrieval of the required information. By 'doubling up' and providing both, we increase the chances of recall. In addition, having a permanent store (the visual image created) to refer back to means that less memory space is taken up.

7. Offer frequent pauses for the learner to process the information required. This will allow the learner time to rehearse what needs to be recalled and to make a more permanent store using their episodic buffer.

8. Strip back. Decide on what the most important 'takeaway' from the lesson is. What exactly do you want the learner to remember? Focus on that, cut out any extraneous information and signpost the key information as a 'red-flag' moment. This helps the learner to concentrate on the most important part of the lesson.

9. Offer a voice recording device. These can be used in a number of supportive ways, such as the following:

   - The learner can record the sentence/content that they need to record. They can then play this back as many times as needed while recording and check for accuracy at the end.

   - The teacher can record verbal instructions when issuing them to the whole class and then give the device to the learner so that they can replay instructions as many times as needed at any point in the task.

10. Make it okay to forget to lessen stress and anxiety. When we feel stressed or anxious, we are more likely to forget. You could agree a discreet 'I've forgotten' signal, so that you know when the learner needs support.

11. Practise retrieval skills using memory games. This can work well – but be careful that the learner does not just get better at playing the game. To support them in developing a set of skills that are transferable to the classroom, engage in metacognitive thinking. Draw their attention to the specific skill that they are developing and explore how it can be utilised in the classroom.

12. Task slice – break larger tasks into smaller steps and offer a supporting visual. As a result, the process of the task will take up less space in the learner's working memory, meaning that they have greater capacity for learning the lesson content.

An example is outlined below.

I need to sequence instructions to show how to make a sandwich in the correct order					
Step 1		Step 2		Step 3	Finished
Cut out all of the instructions.		Place them in the right order on the page in my book.		Check that they are right and stick them in.	
Five minutes		Ten minutes		Five minutes	

Images by FreePik

13. Make sure that the learner feels regulated so that they are 'available' for receiving information. This could involve sensory fidget tools, grounding and breathing activities or opportunities to indicate that they need some time out to refresh.

14. Offer specific rehearsal time for the learner to repeat information to themselves or reproduce it in an alternative format. This will help them to process the information given.

There are lots of tools to choose from. If you are supporting a colleague, it may be helpful to share the following five top tips to take away and try.

	Working memory - five top tips
	When planning lessons, evaluate the working memory demands of learning activities. Consider how much of a burden the process of completing the task will place on the working memory and reduce as many of these demands as possible with supportive tools.
	Offer external tools that can hold information for the learner to revisit as needed – for example: • a voice recording device; • a visual aide memoir; or • a task timeline. This could form a personal memory device toolbox.
	Making forgeting okay. Agree a discreet 'I've forgotten' signal that the learner can make when needed. This will enable you to know that the learner needs support without them feeling embarrassed or different from their peers.
	Pre-teach new content, rehearse skills and/or preview new material and resources before meeting the learner in the lesson. We are more likely to engage with things that we have a previous connection to. This also provides a valuable chance to rehearse retreival.
	Support verbal information and/or instructions with a visual and permanent reminder, such as: • jottings; • a checklist; • a flowchart; • an illustration; or • a diagram. This works effectively as when we learn new information, we store it as an image or a word. By 'doubling up' to provide both, we increase the chances of recall. In addition, having a permanent store (the visual image created) to refer back to means that less memory space is taken up.

Images by FreePik

In addition, parents and caregivers often ask for more information about the difficulties that their child is experiencing. Here is a guide that you can share that will inform them about working memory:

Working memory – a quick guide

What is it?

In its least complex form, 'memory' can be described as the continuous process of information retention over time. It plays a crucial role in learning in the classroom, as learners need to recall what they have previously learned and build on this to develop their knowledge, skills and understanding. There are lots of different types of memory, which include working memory.

Working memory acts as a temporary store that allows us to keep information in mind while we work with it without losing track of the task at hand. Once we have used the information, we forget it because we no longer need it. Working memory can be described as being a bit like a Post-it note. We often jot down things that we have to do on a Post-it note as an impermanent reminder. Once the task is done, we put the Post-it note in the bin and the information is gone forever.

Learners use working memory in the classroom practically all of the time. They need to retain important information while they work on it in the face of distractions from classmates, wall displays, background noise and their own needs, thoughts and feelings.

How can you support your child's working memory?

1. Encourage your child to make a visual image of what they need to remember. They could visualise or, better still, draw a picture of what they need to recall.

2. Make instructions short and simple. Give them one at a time and in the correct sequence of actions to follow.

3. Make it okay to forget. Agree a discreet 'I've forgotten' signal so that your child begins to recognise and you know when they need some support.

4. Break down bigger tasks into smaller steps. Give each step one at a time and think about how you can support each step with a visual cue. This could be a gesture or a picture.

5. Encourage your child to repeat what they need to do.

6. Teach them to create voice notes on their device/mobile phone so that they can replay information as often as is needed.

7. Make new information as familiar and as personally motivating as possible.

Images by FreePik

Finally, the following are three supportive skill builder activities which can be used to support your learners to develop their working memory skills.

Working memory – skill builders

The following activities are all designed to help your learner hold information in mind while working on a task. When completing these activities, it is important to draw specific attention to:

- the skill that they are using;
- why it works; and
- how the skill can be transferred back to the classroom.

The matching pairs game	You will need cards that contain matching pairs of pictures.
	The objective of the game is to collect the most pairs of cards. Shuffle the cards and lay them on the table, face down. This can be in rows or a random shape. On each turn, a player turns over any two cards (one at a time) and keeps them if the pictures on the cards match. If they successfully match a pair, they get to keep the cards and they get another turn. When a player turns over two cards that do not match, those cards are turned face down again (in the same position) and it becomes the next player's turn. The trick is to remember which cards are where while others take their turn. The person with the most pairs at the end of the game wins.
The suitcase game	This is a round-the-table memory game. In a group, go around in turn and say what you are putting in the suitcase. Each person has to say all the other items said previously, as well as adding their own new item. If you get it wrong, you're out! To keep things fresh, decide on a theme for the objects – it doesn't always have to be travel-based.
	To add a level of challenge, include a distraction before the person whose turn it is can respond or a task to complete at the same time, such as colouring or a word search.
The tray game	Place a number of items on a tray and ask learners to look at it for 20 seconds. Cover the tray with a cloth or other barrier and give them 30 seconds to write down everything can be remembered from the tray. For a variation of this game, select a learner, or group of learners, to look away (or leave the room). Remove one or several items from the tray and have them guess what has changed. To add a level of challenge, delay the learners before they have chance to record what they can remember from the tray.

Images by FreePik

Do you remember Sam from the working memory case study earlier in the chapter?

REFLECTION POINT

- Which tools would you consider using to help Sam if he were in your class?
- What impact would you hope to see?

TABLE 2.1 Sam's revised provision

Support	Impact	Suggested next step
Tabletop copy of resources that need to be copied	Greater accuracy in copying but Sam still works slowly – letter by letter.	Evaluate the task: does Sam really need to copy the information into his book? Could he stick a pre-prepared version in and read through it, highlighting the important parts for later revision? If the information must be copied, could it be 'chunked' into smaller 'bite-sized' pieces?
Task slicing – breaking tasks into smaller stages and issuing them one at a time	This works well as long as a visual timeline is provided.	Ensure that the visual timeline is always available to Sam. Use an arrow that he can move to indicate his placement within the task.
Basic skills catch-up programme	At times, Sam makes huge leaps forwards but then seems to regress. His recall is very variable on a day-to-day basis.	Strip this back to the bare essentials, with dedicated time for retrieval practice. Ensure that he gets to apply his new skills in the classroom learning context.
Memory games	Sam gets better at playing the game so he recalls more, but this does not seem to transfer as a skill back into his work in the classroom.	Introduce a metacognitive element that helps Sam to identify: • the exact skills that he is learning; • why the games work well for him; and • where and when he can use these skills in the classroom.
Timeout card	Sam uses this well when he becomes overloaded/overwhelmed and visits the classroom 'chillout zone'. He returns to the group once he has self-regulated.	Introduce self-regulation tools that he can use in a proactive sense to stay regulated in the classroom learning experience, such as sensory fidget tools and/or grounding and breathing activities. This may lessen trips to the 'chillout zone'.

Considering all the tools suggested, Sam's provision has been reviewed and some new suggestions made. You will see that the suggestions either refine what is already on offer or add a simple further idea. Tiny tweaks can make a significant difference.

CHAPTER TAKEAWAYS

- In its least complex form, 'memory' can be described as the continuous process of information retention over time. Memory is an essential part of human cognition since it permits us to remember previous events to aid our understanding and behaviour in the present.
- Working memory acts as a temporary store that allows us to keep information in mind while we work with it without losing track of the task at hand. Once we have used the information, we forget it because we no longer need it. If we retain it, it just takes up valuable space.
- In the classroom, learners use their working memory for many routine tasks, as well as the business of learning. Many of these tasks place a burden on working memory, as the learner is required to hold some information in mind while engaging in effortful activity.

Chapter 3
SELF-MONITORING

What is it?

Self-monitoring is a crucial part of executive functioning. It is our ability to actively observe and evaluate our own thoughts, feelings and emotions and then adjust using strategies to adapt our behaviour so that we can access the task and achieve a goal. It provides a helpful 'self-check' mechanism. Self-monitoring also enables us to identify and resolve errors in our work or to modify our approach to support the achievement of a successful outcome or goal. To achieve that goal, whether it be directed by the teacher or self-chosen, our learners need to achieve and maintain a regulated state so that they remain 'available' for learning.

When we consider the concept of being in a regulated state and feeling available for learning, it can be helpful to think of Goldilocks and her visit to the home of the three bears. When trying out the porridge, chairs and beds, it was important to Goldilocks that each one was 'just right'. For successful learning to happen, it is essential that our learners feel 'just right' so that they can achieve a state of optimal cognitive function. This encompasses using strategies to reduce the distractions that are potentially caused by strong emotions, leading to improved focus and concentration on learning and the facilitation of positive interactions with teachers and other learners. These are all essential to achieving classroom success.

Self-monitoring can be presented as a cycle:

> **REFLECTION POINT**
> - Can you identify any learners who may be experiencing difficulties with self-monitoring in your classroom?
> - What do these look like?
> - What impact do they have on their ability to access learning?

DOI: 10.4324/9781003534075-3

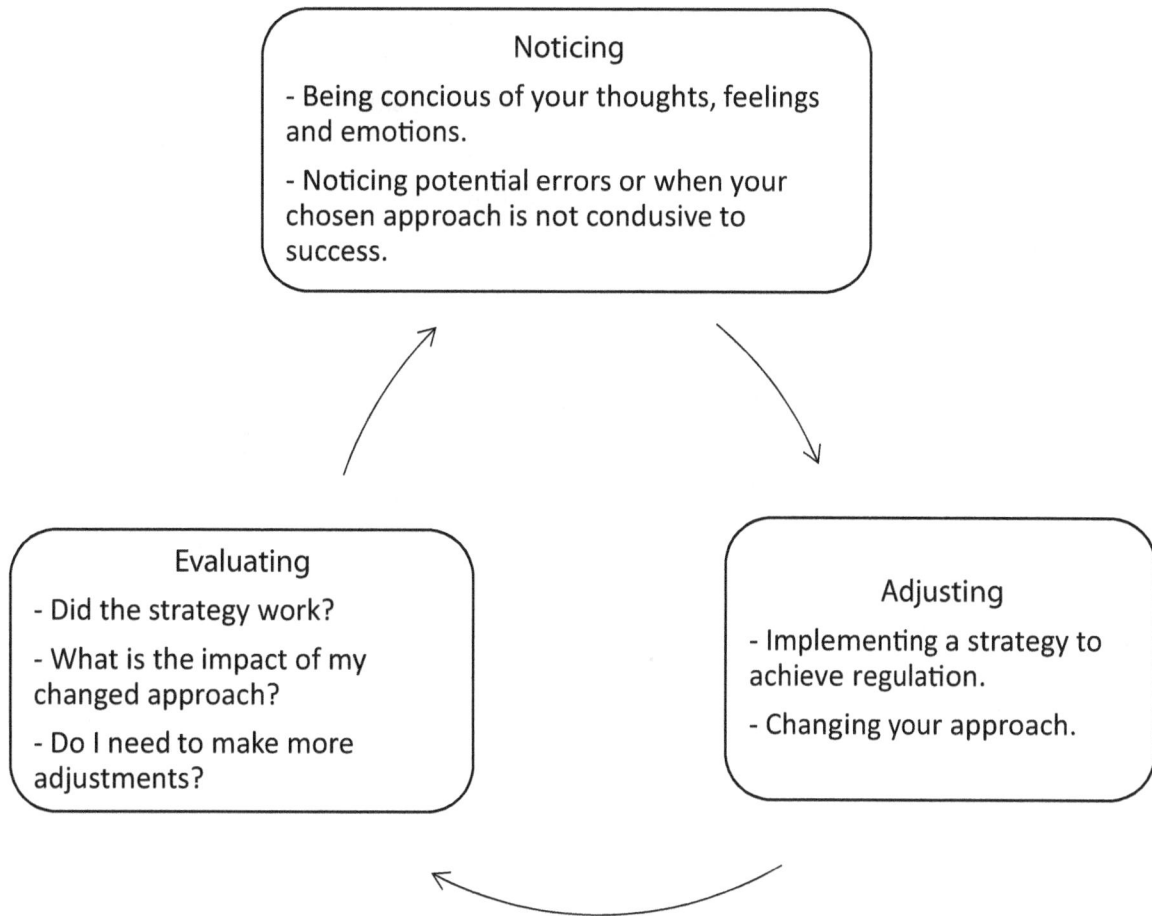

FIGURE 3.1 A self-monitoring cycle

Self-monitoring and classroom success

Imagine that you are a learner who has been asked to paint a portrait of your best friend. In the lead-up to this task, your teacher has provided opportunities for you to look at portraits painted by favourite artists, you have taken photographs of your friend to use as source material and you have mixed exactly the right colours to work with. You are all good to go!

As you begin painting, you notice that you feel thirsty and hot, and that the person sitting next to you is producing a better painting than you. No matter how hard you try, you just can't seem to get the eyes on your portrait to be the right shape or to line up just how you want them to. Your legs are beginning to twitch as you can feel the frustration mounting. You are becoming dysregulated and less available to access the task. It is at this crucial point that you need to stop, take note of all that is happening and adjust so that you can re-regulate yourself and get back to the task. This needs to be done proactively before you are completely dysregulated and unable to learn.

As you are an experienced learner with good self-monitoring skills, you spot the thirstiness, hotness, envy, twitching legs and growing frustration – and pause. In that moment, you make the decision to get up, visit the bathroom, remove your school jumper, take a deep breath and ask a friend how they managed to get the eyes on their portrait perfect. This helps you to feel 'just right'. You make the most of this Goldilocks moment and return to the task successfully.

On this occasion, your ability to do these things impacted directly on your classroom success and whether the goal of producing a portrait of your best friend was achieved.

REFLECTION POINT
- Can you recall a time when you had to make adjustments to your state to achieve and maintain a regulated state?
- What did you do in this situation?
- How did it help?

Often, learners with self-monitoring difficulties might:

- experience difficulties with identifying their own feelings;
- find it challenging to identify what is and is not working well;
- continue with a task in the same way even if they are not succeeding;
- find it hard to self-assess strengths and areas to develop;
- fail to spot errors in their own work;
- appear to be copying or checking their own actions against what their peers are doing;
- present as reluctant to seek support from others;
- not use provided scaffolding resources;
- not check their own work;
- find it hard to notice and then respond to social cues from peers; and
- demonstrate sensory-seeking/sensory-avoiding behaviours which may support self-regulation.

REFLECTION POINT

- Can you think of a learner in your classroom who presents with these difficulties?
- How do their difficulties manifest themselves as barriers to learning?

Here is a case study which illustrates a learner who experiences self-monitoring challenges.

Self-monitoring in the classroom – a case study

Background information

Aminah is working at age-related expectations all subjects. Her progress across the curriculum is rapid at times and can then plateau for lengthy periods.

It can be difficult to predict Aminah's mood, which can change rapidly and often unexpectedly. She frequently falls out with her friends and seems to get frustrated quickly when something does not go according to her plan.

Aminah's previous teachers describe her as being rigid in her thinking. She has a particular way in which she likes to approach a task and will stick with this regardless of how successful it is. This can cause difficulties when approaching problem-solving tasks.

The usual reward charts and a high level of adult modelling of a range of approaches to problem solving have being trialled with little positive and sustained impact.

Information from the class teacher

Aminah's teacher reports that she is a 'very lovely girl', but that her growing frustration and angry outbursts in lessons are becoming more challenging to manage. Aminah will often abandon a task as she feels that she just cannot complete it. Often, she will leave the room when she becomes overwhelmed because of not achieving success quickly.

Observations

Mathematics: making nets to construct a three-dimensional shape

Aminah was able to identify which nets would make which three-dimensional shapes confidently. She smiled as she received praise for doing so and enjoyed helping peers who were finding this task challenging. When asked to make a net that would construct a cube, Aminah started well. She understood the placement of the squares. However, she did not realise that she would have to add on tabs for the squares to stick together. When she had cut out her net and it would not stick together, she screwed it up and threw it on the floor.

Science: constructing an electrical circuit to light up a bulb

Aminah understood that the goal was to get the bulb to light up and was able to collect all the correct elements required to make a circuit. When making her circuit, Aminah experienced difficulties with connecting the battery correctly using the crocodile clips provided. She continually adopted the same approach, which resulted in the battery and the wire coming apart. After five attempts, Aminah pushed her circuit away and got up and left the classroom. An adult followed her to ensure that she was safe.

Support and impact to date

Support	Impact
Provision of a red, green and amber card to show how she feels about the task: • Red: The task is too difficult. I need help right now. • Amber: The task is challenging but I will be able to do it. • Green: The task is easy. No help is needed.	Aminah uses the cards sometimes – often only the red one. When this card is used, it is important that an adult is quick to meet her needs. If Aminah is left waiting for support, she can quickly become dysregulated and will leave the room.
A resilience-building intervention. Aminah has worked in a group of four with a teaching assistant rehearsing critical thinking skills. In this intervention, the learners are shown how to follow a process in which they: • identify the problem; • identify what existing skills they have which will help; • make a plan; • execute the plan and adapt the plan accordingly as they work towards solving the problem; and • evaluate their success, explicitly citing which skills they used.	Aminah can follow this process when coached by the teaching assistant in the group. However, she is yet to transfer these skills to tasks in the classroom.
Aminah has a self-monitoring chart which is available for her to use in every lesson. This chart allows her to pick and signal one of three emotions: happy, sad and angry. Each emotion is accompanied by a matching facial expression and a list of self-help strategies to support the achievement of a regulated state.	Aminah can identify and responds appropriately to happy and sad. She finds the more finely graded emotions in between these difficult. She can describe how her body feels when she is happy or sad and connects this to the emotion.
Aminah has a timeout card which she can use when she feels that she requires a five-minute break from a task when she identifies signs of frustration.	Aminah has had several of these cards but often rips them up when she is frustrated. She appears to lack the skills to be proactive in using the cards. Often, it is too late.

Next steps

Aminah's behaviours are increasing and her mood changes rapidly and unpredictably. It is appropriate to consider whether one-to-one support from a learning mentor is required, together with the development of a more specific behaviour management plan.

Aminah is clearly struggling. The following toolkit contains strategies that can support her and other learners who experience the same self-monitoring difficulties.

Self-monitoring toolkit

Classroom challenges
• Experience difficulties with identifying their own feelings;
• Find it challenging to identify what is and is not working well;
• Continue with a task in the same way even if they are not succeeding;
• Find it hard to self-assess strengths and areas to develop;
• Fail to spot errors in their own work;
• Appear to be copying or checking their own actions against what their peers are doing;
• Present as reluctant to seek support from others;
• Fail to use provided scaffolding resources;
• Fail to check their own work;
• Find it hard to notice and then respond to social cues from peers; and
• Demonstrate sensory-seeking/sensory-avoiding behaviours which may support self-regulation.

Tools

1 Support the learner to make a link between how their body feels or is acting and their emotions by wondering aloud. Here are some example phrases:

'I can see that your cheeks are looking red and you are clenching your teeth. I wonder if that means you could be feeling angry?'

'When my tummy feels a bit like a washing machine and my heart beats fast, it means that I am worrying. I wonder if that is the same for you?'

When the learner can do this, you can then add the suggestion of a self-help strategy. For example:

'When my tummy feels a bit like a washing machine and my heart beats fast, it means that I am worrying. When this happens, I tell a friend what is making me feel like this. Do you think that could work for you?'

2 When beginning a new learning activity/approach, support the learner to identify existing skills and strengths that they can transfer to the task. Work on developing metacognition skills would support this.

3 Develop a place for the learner to note down worries about the task so that they can be addressed at an appropriate time.

4 Develop a structured script to approach problem-solving based tasks:

   • What is the problem?

   • What are all the things that I can do to handle it?

   • What will happen if I do each of those things?

   • Which way of handling it is the best?

   • Now that I have tried it, how did I do?

   • Could I do anything differently next time?

5 Model and celebrate 'failure' and making mistakes as a way of learning that can lead to a positive outcome.

6   Work with the learner to develop a self-monitoring and regulation check-in with accompanying strategies. Here is an example that was coproduced with a Year 4 learner:

Emotion	How it feels for me	What it looks like when I feel this way	'I can' strategies (What can I do?)	'You can' strategies (How can others help me?)
Happy	• Still. • I want to smile and laugh. • My heart beats like it should. • Like when I have ice-cream.	• I am smiling. • I am glowing. • I am working and joining in.	• Enjoy the feeling. • Think about the good things that I am doing and how I can keep doing them.	• Notice and celebrate with me.
Angry	• Hot. • My heart is going fast. • My head feels full. • I feel like I am going to burst.	• I have a red face. • I clench my fists. • I bang on the table. • I start swinging my legs.	• Stop and do a breathing activity. • Use my words to say why I am angry. • Use my timeout card.	• Offer me a drink to help me cool down. • Use one of my distraction activities like colouring until I feel less angry. • Stamp my feet and clap my hands loudly.
Frustrated	• Everything is too much to handle and I can't do it anymore.	• I am twitchy. • I am not joining in with the work or with my friends.	• Ask for help. • Stop the task, use one of my sensory tools and then go back to it.	• Notice and ask whether I need help. • Show me what to do again. • Remind me of my strengths and the things that I can do.
Sad	• Empty. • I don't want to join in anymore.	• Tears. • My eyes are closing. • I am on my own because I don't want others near me.	• Write or draw about what has made me upset and share it with my trusted adult. • Think a happy thought.	• Guide me to go to my safe space. • Ask whether I am okay, but not in front of everyone else. • Give me a tissue and offer me a drink of water.

7   Developing critical thinking skills by taking an 'assess, plan, do, review' approach:

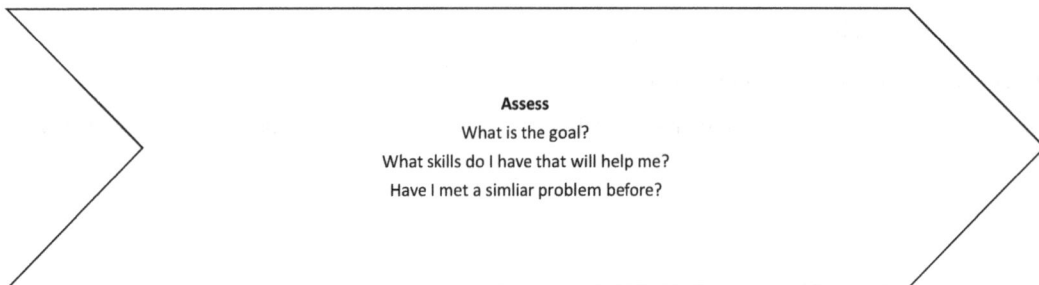

Assess
What is the goal?
What skills do I have that will help me?
Have I met a simliar problem before?

8   Provide a tabletop 'hints and tips' card with suggested strategies to problem solve. For example:

What can I do if I am stuck?

- Check back in my workbook.
- Use a dictionary.
- Ask a friend.
- Look at the working wall for a clue.
- Ask my teacher for a clue.

9   Pause the lesson/task and ask the learners to specifically consider the following:

- How do they think the task is going?
- What skills have they already got that they are using?
- What is going well?
- What do they wish was going better?
- How near to achieving their goal are they?
- What could they try to improve their performance?
- What resources are available to use that might help?

Some learners will find it have helpful to have a bank of sentence stems to begin their answers to these questions. Some learners might like to work through these prompts with a peer partner.

10 Rehearse 'reading' and wondering aloud about real-life scenarios, exploring what can be seen and what could be appropriate responses. For example:

'I can see that this person is in pain because they are crying and holding their ankle. I wonder why that could be? Perhaps they have hurt themselves. What could we do?'

11 Break down larger tasks into smaller steps to avoid overwhelm.

12 Use a traffic-light system for learners to grade the task according to how they feel about it. Support and encouragement can then be matched to the learner's self-assessment.

13 Offer opportunities for learners to 'think, pair, share' (a collaborative learning strategy where students individually 'think' about a question, topic or task; 'pair' with a partner to discuss and develop their ideas; and then 'share' their thoughts with the class). This allows for self and peer evaluation of their understanding.

14 Develop self-assessment checklists or rubrics for students to self-mark against. As they become more skilled at this, they can set their own marking criteria.

15 Explore the learner's sensory needs considering what sorts of calming and alerting sensory experiences help them to achieve a regulated state. This could develop into a sensory toolbox containing sensory tools for the learners to use when required. These could include fidget tools, scent from a perfume/aftershave sample, weighted tools and ideas for movement breaks.

16 Use search cards to encourage self-checking and editing. A search card is a teacher-prepared resource that is given to the learner when they have completed their work to guide them towards what might need checking and editing. This can be a simple Post-it note. For example:

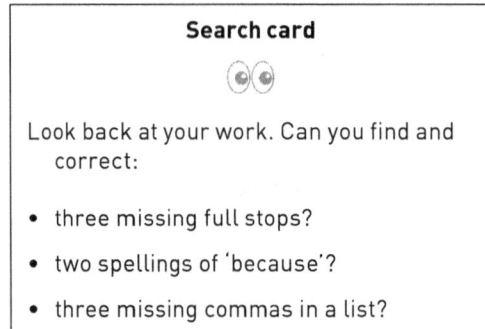

> **Search card**
>
> 👀
>
> Look back at your work. Can you find and correct:
>
> - three missing full stops?
>
> - two spellings of 'because'?
>
> - three missing commas in a list?

As your learner becomes more secure with this approach, you can encourage them to identify an error and correct independently.

Images by Freepik

If you are supporting a colleague, it may be helpful to give them five top tips to take away and try. Here is something that you can share with them:

	Self-monitoring – five top tips
	Wonder aloud to help the learner connect their physiology to the feeling – for example: 'I can see that your legs are twitching and your face is getting red. You look close to crying. I wonder if this is because you are feeling frustrated with this task?'
	Offer sensory tools that help the learner to achieve a regulated state. These could include: • a range of fidget tools; • alerting or relaxing scents; • ideas for movement breaks; and • a weight lap-pad. These should be personal to the learner and based on what works well to alert or calm them.
	Develop a traffic-light system so that the learner can grade their perceived difficulty of a task. Support can then be matched accordingly.
	Develop a problem-solving script so that the learner has a safety net of stages to work through. As part of this script, encourage them to consider what skills, strengths and talents they already have and can utilise to work towards success.
	Develop a personalised self-monitoring and regulation chart that the learner can use to identify how they are feeling and what strategies they can use to either enjoy that feeling or change their state.

Images by Freepik

Parents and caregivers might ask for more information about the self-monitoring-related challenges that their child is experiencing. Here is something that you can share that will provide them with further information.

Self-monitoring - a quick guide

What is it?

Self-monitoring is our ability to actively observe and evaluate our own thoughts, feelings and emotions and then use strategies to adapt our behaviour so that we can access the task and achieve a goal. It provides a helpful 'self-check' mechanism. Self-monitoring also enables us to identify and resolve errors in our work or to modify our approach to support the achievement of a successful outcome or goal.

Children who find it hard to self-monitor might:

- experience difficulties with identifying their own feelings;

- find it challenging to identify what is and is not working well;

- continue with a task in the same way even if they are not succeeding;

- find it hard to self-assess strengths and areas to develop;

- fail to spot errors in their own work;

- appear to be copying or checking their own actions against what their peers are doing;

- present as reluctant to seek support from others;

- not use provided scaffolding resources;

- not check their own work;

- find it hard to notice and then respond to social cues from peers; and

- demonstrate sensory-seeking/sensory-avoiding behaviours which may support self-regulation.

How can you support your child to develop self-monitoring skills?

1 Wonder aloud so that they can connect the way that their body feels to their emotions – for example: 'I can see that your cheeks are looking red and you are clenching your teeth. I wonder if that means you could be feeling angry?'

2 Develop a structured script to approach problem-solving based tasks:

- What is the problem?

- What are all the things that I can do to handle it?

- What will happen if I do each of those things?

- Which way of handling it is the best?

- Now that I have tried it, how did I do?

- Can I do anything differently next time?

3 Model and celebrate 'failure' and making mistakes as a way of learning that can lead to a positive outcome.

Images by Freepik

Finally, here are three supportive skill builder activities which can be used to support your learners to develop self-monitoring skills.

<table>
<tr><td colspan="2">Self-monitoring - skill builders</td></tr>
<tr><td colspan="2">The following activities are designed to help your learner to develop self-monitoring skills. When completing these activities, it is important to draw specific attention to:

• the skill that they are using;

• why it works; and

• how the skill can be transferred back to the classroom.</td></tr>
<tr><td>Assess, plan, do, review</td><td>Set your learner a critical thinking task in which they must solve a problem. In solving the task, they must complete the following steps:

• Assess: What do I need to do and what useful skills do I already have?

• Plan: Make a plan.

• Do: Implement the plan and make adjustments as you go along.

• Review: Did the plan work? What did we learn? What went well?</td></tr>
<tr><td>Traffic-light system</td><td>Use a traffic-light system to help your learner to grade the activity according to their perception of how difficult the task is. Support can then be provided at an appropriate level.</td></tr>
<tr><td>Wonder together</td><td>Look at real-life scenarios and wonder together – for example: 'I can see that this person is in pain because they are crying and holding their ankle. I wonder why that could be? Perhaps they have hurt themselves. What could we do?'</td></tr>
</table>

Images designed by FreePik

So, back to Aminah from our self-monitoring case study.

REFLECTION POINT

• Which three tools would you consider learning to help Aminah if she were in your class?

• What impact would you hope to see?

Using the self-monitoring toolkit, the following strategies were deployed. In Table 3.1 on the next page you can see their impact:

TABLE 3.1 Aminah's revised provision

Support	Impact	Suggested next step
Wondering aloud.	Aminah is now beginning to make the connection between her physiology (the way her body feels) and her emotions.	Continue this approach to consolidate and embed. Once secure, consider adding a suggested management strategy – for example: 'If your body is telling you that you are feeling angry, you could …'
Use of a traffic-light system for Aminah to grade how difficult she believes an activity to be.	Aminah uses this strategy well. Often, she is grading activities as 'amber', meaning that she will 'have a go'.	Encourage Aminah to respond to changes in her perception proactively – for example, showing red if she feels that things are becoming too difficult.
Use of a structured script to approach a problem.	Aminah now approaches tasks with greater confidence and independence, as she can identify existing strengths before the task commences and when a problem arises.	Encourage Aminah to identify why a task was successful. Challenge her to consider what she did that resulted in success.

CHAPTER TAKEAWAYS

- Self-monitoring is a crucial part of executive functioning. It acts a useful 'self-check.' It can be described as our ability to actively observe and evaluate our own thoughts, feelings and emotions and then use strategies to adjust our behaviour so that we can access the task and achieve a goal.
- Often, learners with self-monitoring difficulties might:
    - experience difficulties with identifying their own feelings;
    - find it challenging to identify what is and is not working well;
    - continue with a task in the same way even if they are not succeeding;
    - find it hard to self-assess strengths and areas to develop;
    - fail to spot errors in their own work;
    - appear to be copying or checking their own actions against what their peers are doing;
    - present as reluctant to seek support from others;
    - not use provided scaffolding resources;
    - not check their own work;
    - find it hard to notice and then respond to social cues from peers;
    - demonstrate sensory-seeking/sensory-avoiding behaviours which may support self-regulation.
- Several strategies can be deployed to support learners with self-monitoring difficulties, such as:
    - wondering aloud to encourage self-reflection so that the learner can link their physiology to their feelings; and
    - grading the perceived difficulty of activities so that the appropriate level of support can be provided.

Chapter 4

PLANNING AND PRIORITISING

What is it?

The ability to plan and prioritise effectively is a key cognitive skill that forms part of our executive functions. Planning and prioritising involve creating a useful roadmap that will lead you towards achieving an end goal. To do this effectively, our learners need to be able to see into the future to determine what 'finished' will look like – and then break down their vision into the manageable steps needed to arrive there. Once this is done, the learner needs to decide which tasks are the most important to focus on first and what order everything else should come in. They will then be able to manage their time and workload efficiently and effectively. Within this, at the task maintenance stage, we must also consider the ability to place keep – that is, to know where you are within the stages of a task and what you will need to do next.

When we think more about planning and prioritising skills, a parallel can be drawn to cooking a Sunday roast dinner. Knowing what the final plate of food served will contain is just the first step. To arrive at the end goal of dinner on the plate, we must then consider the following:

- what ingredients we require and whether we already have them or whether they need purchasing;
- how many people we are cooking for;
- how much we will need of each ingredient;
- what will need preparing and how this will be done – for example, peeling the potatoes ready to roast;

DOI: 10.4324/9781003534075-4

- what time dinner will be served at;
- how long the ingredients will need cooking for in relation to each other;
- what time the plates will need warming at;
- the order in which each ingredient will be placed on the plate;
- when the table will be laid; and
- what extra condiments will be needed for serving.

You can see that the task isn't as simple as just cooking!

REFLECTION POINT

- Can you think of a daily task that you have to complete which relies heavily on your ability to plan and prioritise effectively?
- What can go wrong if the planning and prioritising involved in this task are not effective?

Planning and prioritising and classroom success

Planning and prioritising are essential classroom skills. Without them, we would be unable to begin and complete the work required to achieve success in the classroom or manage the demands of homework.

Daily, we ask our learners to write the date and title of an exercise in their workbooks. On the surface, this could be viewed as a relatively simple task for most of the learners in your class. It forms part of the many embedded routines that we establish in the early days of classroom instruction. However, the level of planning and prioritising required to get this done within a given time to be ready for learning can pose a challenge for many. Let's break down this task so that we can see just what is involved.

The end goal
To have copied the date and title of the exercise accurately from the board into your workbook in five minutes, ready to start work.

TABLE 4.1 Breaking down a task

The stages
Stage 1: Ensure that you have the correct writing tool and workbook.
Stage 2: Assess how much time you have.
Stage 3: Decide what needs to be copied first – will it be the date or the title?
Stage 4: Look at the board for the first letter.
Stage 5: Hold that letter in mind and then look at the book.
Stage 6: Write down the first letter.
Stage 7: Repeat Stages 4-6 for all other letters, checking the available time as you go and speeding up if necessary.
Stage 8: Check that the task has been accurately completed.
Stage 9: Put down your writing tool to show your teacher that you are ready.

REFLECTION POINT

- What could pose potential difficulties with this task if the learner finds planning and prioritising challenging?

There are several ways in which this task could go wrong due to difficulties with planning and prioritising – for example:

- the learner may start in the incorrect place, leading to a jumbled date and title;
- they may misjudge the time available and thus not finish or even begin the task;
- they may lose their place within the task, leading to spelling errors and/or missed information; or
- they may prioritise a totally different task, such as sharpening their pencil or reading a book.

For some learners, what we may consider to be a simple and embedded daily classroom task can cause a feeling of overwhelm. Is it any wonder that these learners often do not begin a task, become easily sidetracked or engage in prolonged procrastination?

Learners who experience difficulties with planning and prioritising might:

- find it challenging to think ahead;
- often see the end result but be unable to identify the steps required to get to this;

- appear to be disorganised;
- appear to be impulsive;
- not consider the future consequences of their immediate actions;
- not have the correct resources for a task; and
- appear to always be in the 'here and now'.

Without support in school, the crucial life and employability skills of project management, meeting deadlines, decision making and adapting to evolving situations will be much harder to develop.

REFLECTION POINT

- Can you think of a learner who experiences difficulties with planning and prioritising?
- What do their difficulties look like in your learning environment?

Here is another real-life case study which illustrates the sorts of difficulties that a learner may have in the classroom.

Planning and prioritising in the classroom – a case study

Background information

Jude is working at significantly below age-related expectations in all subjects. His progress is described as sporadic, as consistent retention of prior learning is a significant issue.

Jude often knows what he needs to do and what 'finished' looks like, but he struggles to get there. Without direct adult intervention in lessons, he achieves very little in terms of productivity.

A speech and language assessment evidenced that he does not have a receptive language difficulty. His annual school reports have a historical theme in which he is described as articulate and with a sound understanding of concepts.

Information from the class teacher

Jude's workbooks are full of incomplete and abandoned work, yet he is on task for the whole lesson. He often muddles or forgets the stages in a process, which can make solving more complex mathematical problems or carrying out the steps to complete a scientific investigation problematic. Jude's written work does not reflect the true level of his knowledge and understanding. Generally, when executing a classroom task, he either can appear be impulsive or is slow to get going without direct adult intervention.

Observations

Mathematics: solving two-step word problems

Jude read each word problem carefully and was able to independently identify which of the four operations was required to solve the given word problems. However, when it came to solving the problems, Jude found it very difficult to follow the two-step process required. He encountered a range of difficulties, including:

- only solving the first or last part of the question;
- missing out a stage in an equation;
- dealing with the information given in the correct order; and
- time management – in 20 minutes, he completed just three questions, which were all only partially correct.

Reading: reading a non-chronological report and providing a written answer to related comprehension questions

Jude made several excellent and accurate contributions during the lesson introduction in which the class completed a shared reading of a text and the teacher modelled how to skim and scan a text to locate information to answer comprehension questions. When sent to work independently on a similar task, Jude found it difficult to approach the task in an organised manner. He initially read some of the comprehension questions and then spent time looking at the illustrations that accompanied the text. He then read the last paragraph of the text and answered one of the questions. The teacher spotted that Jude was experiencing some difficulties, so approached him and asked him to pause. Together, they co-constructed what the process should look like through careful questioning – for example, what should you do first? The teacher used Jude's answers to create a simple checklist on a mini whiteboard for him to follow. This worked well as Jude followed the process meticulously through to the end, with the support of frequent time checks related to productivity from his teacher.

Support and impact to date

Support	Impact
Adult-supported organisation in the form of careful questioning to support Jude in eliciting what he should do first, then, next and last.	With specific and careful prompting, Jude can identify the steps in a task. However, if left to his own devices, he is unable to do this independently, which results in disorganised attempts to complete a task.
Use of a visual task timeline.	Jude will follow a given visual timeline but needs frequent time and productivity-based adult-led checklists to keep him going to the end.
Partial completion activities to support Jude in not having to do all of a given process.	Jude can usually complete the part required. The next step is for him to take on more than one step of a process.

Next steps

Working on developing independent task-slicing and completion skills. At present, Jude is very heavily reliant on adults to do this for him.

There are several tools which could be effective in supporting Jude. The following toolkit details many of these.

Planning and prioritising toolkit

Classroom challenges
• Find it challenging to think ahead;
• Can often see the end result but cannot identify the steps required to get to this;
• Appear to be disorganised;
• Appear to be impulsive;
• Do not consider the future consequences of their immediate actions;
• Do not have the correct resources for a task; and
• Appear to always be in the 'here and now'.

Tools

1 Offer a task-slicing approach. Task slicing is the act of breaking down a large task into smaller, more manageable steps, allowing for a more focused and efficient approach to completing the work. This can take many forms, such as a to-do list or a simple visual task timeline. Motivators and rewards can be built into this process – for example:

Step 1		Step 2	Step 3	Step 4	Step 5	Step 6	Finished
Read the text.	⭐	Read the first question.	Decide what information I need to find.	Skim and scan to find the information in the text.	Use the information to decide on my answer.	Write down my answer.	🏆

Time prompts can also be added to show how long to spend on each element of the task.

2 Use a traffic-light system to help the learner to prioritise tasks. Red tasks can wait; amber tasks need doing, but not right now; and green tasks must be done immediately.
3 Provide the learner with a blank flow chart to populate so that they can divide large tasks into smaller tasks and subdivide them further if necessary:

4 Teach time-blocking skills and techniques so that the learner can allocate specific time slots for specific tasks.
5 Provide a completed example or finished model and help the learner to work backwards from that point.
6 Provide resource checklists so that the learner can fetch and organise their own resources efficiently. This could be in written or pictorial format.
7 Use an in and out-tray system so that the learner has a clear idea of what they need to do and what they have completed. This will support place keeping and general task organisation.
8 Set aside dedicated planning time before the learner is asked to begin a task.
9 Offer graded procedural worked examples which build familiarity with a process before full task handover takes place – for example:

The learner is given a task which requires them to complete three steps			
The adult models all three steps.	The adult completes Steps 1 and 2. The learner completes Step 3.	The adult completes Steps 1. The learner completes Steps 2 and 3.	The learner completes all three steps.
Provision of a worked example to check against.	Completion of Task 1.	Completion of Task 2.	Completion of Task 3.

Lesson starts ⟶ Lesson ends

10 Offer writing frames to help learners organise their ideas into logical categories.

11 Explore cause and effect. Provide your learners with scenarios in which they have to consider two possible outcomes of their actions. Discuss which action will give the best outcome and why.

12 Play games in which learners must think ahead to develop and hold a strategy in mind, such as Connect 4, draughts, Rummikub, Othello, chess and Battleship.

13 When approaching a problem, list all the available solutions – no matter how unrealistic – and then explore which solution might work best and why.

Images by FreePik

REFLECTION POINT

- Which three tools would you consider using to help Jude if he were in your class?
- What impact would you hope to see?

As for the two previous elements of executive functioning, here are five top tips to share with a colleague that they might like to take away and try.

	Planning and prioritising – five top tips
	When planning your lesssons, dedicate specific time for learners to plan what they need to do and to prioritise the tasks.
	When you model how to approach a task, think aloud. This makes the invisible visible and tangible and provides your learners with a model for how they might approach a task.
	Develop a traffic-light system so that learners can colour-code activities. Red means that the task can wait, as it is unimportant; amber means that the task needs be done, but not immediately; and green signals that the task must be done right now. Ask your learners to justify their traffic-light colour choice.
	Task slice: break down large tasks into smaller stages and provide a written to-do list or visual timeline to support place keeping.
	Explore cause and effect. Provide your learners with scenarios in which they have to consider two possible outcomes of their actions. Discuss which action will provide the best outcome and why. This will help them to see into the future so that they know what 'finished' could look like.

Images by FreePik

For parents and caregivers who ask for more information about how to support their child with developing planning and prioritising-related skills, here is some further information that you can share:

Planning and prioritising – a quick guide

What is it?

Planning and prioritising involve creating a useful roadmap which leads towards the achievement of an end goal. To do this effectively, learners need to be able to see into the future to determine what 'finished' will look like – and then break down their vision into manageable steps to arrive there. The learner needs to decide which tasks are the most important to focus on first and what order everything else should come in. Within this, at the task maintenance stage, we must also consider the ability to place keep – that is, to know where you are within the stages of a task and what you will need to do next.

Children who find it hard to plan and prioritise might:

- find it challenging to think ahead;
- be able to see the end result but be unable to identify the steps required to get to this;
- appear to be disorganised;
- appear to be impulsive;
- not consider the future consequences of their immediate actions;
- not have the correct resources for a task; and
- appear to always be in the 'here and now'.

How can you support your child to develop planning and prioritising skills?

1 Play games in which your child must develop and hold a strategy in mind, such as Connect 4, Rummikub, Othello, Guess Who?, chess and Battleship.
2 When approaching everyday tasks such as getting dressed or making a sandwich, rehearse breaking these down into smaller steps and ordering them accordingly. You might like to draw a simple flowchart to illustrate the process.
3 When approaching a problem, list all the available solutions – no matter how unrealistic – and then explore which solution might work best and why.
4 Develop a traffic-light system to help your child colour-code the urgency of a task. Red means that the task can wait; amber indicates that the task needs doing, but not immediately; and green signals that the task must be done right now.

Images by FreePik

Finally, here are three skill builder activities which can be used to support your learners to develop planning and prioritising skills.

Planning and prioritising – skill builders

The following activities are all designed to help your learner to develop their planning and prioritising skills. When completing these activities, it is important to draw specific attention to:

- the skill that they are using;
- why it works; and
- how the skill can be transferred back to the classroom.

Play strategy games	Play games in which learners must develop and hold a strategy in mind, such as Connect 4, Rummikub, Othello, Guess Who?, chess and Battleship. This will encourage then to plan and hold a goal in mind while having fun!
Traffic-light systems	Use a traffic-light system to help your learner to grade the urgency of the tasks that they must complete. They may wish to have a set of paper traffic lights that they can use to write or draw the tasks on to help them to recall their decisions. • Red: This task is not important and can wait a long time. • Amber: This task needs to be done but is not urgent. I can do it within this timescale … • Green: Do it now!
Cause and effect puzzle pieces	Encourage your learner to think ahead by exploring cause and effect. Present them with jigsaw puzzle pieces which pair together, one with the cause and one with the effect – for example: • Cause: I leave a task until the very last minute. • Effect: The task is not completed as I run out of time. The learner must match the pieces together and justify their decision.

Images by FreePik

It's time to check back in on Jude to see how he is getting on. Using the self-monitoring toolkit, the following strategies were deployed. Here you can see their impact:

TABLE 4.2 Jude's revised provision

Support	Impact	Suggested next step
Playing strategy games in which Jude had to develop a strategy to achieve the goal of winning.	Jude was really enthused by this approach. He clearly loves to win! Jude can now confidently articulate the end result (he calls this 'seeing into the future') and is able to describe the steps that he took to win.	Increase the complexity of the games and support Jude to document his strategy before implementing it using a flow chart or visual task slicer. He can then transfer this skill back into the classroom.
Use of a traffic-light system for Jude to colour code tasks according to their urgency.	Jude uses this strategy effectively when prompted. At present, he requires an adult to prompt him to work out what colour to award the task but usually makes a sensible and logical choice. This has led to him approaching three-step tasks in a more logical manner.	Work to secure this as an independent strategy in the classroom.

CHAPTER TAKEAWAYS

- Planning and prioritising involves creating a useful roadmap that leads towards the achievement of an end goal.
- To plan and prioritise effectively, learners need to be able to see into the future to determine what 'finished' will look like – and then break down their vision into manageable steps to arrive there. The learner needs to decide which tasks are the most important to focus on first and what order everything else should come in.
- At the task maintenance stage, we must also consider the ability to place keep – that is, to know where you are within the stages of a task and what you will need to do next.
- Often, learners who experience difficulties with planning and prioritising might:
    - find it challenging to think ahead;
    - be able to see the end result but be unable to identify the steps required to get to this;
    - appear to be disorganised;
    - appear to be impulsive;
    - not consider the future consequences of their immediate actions;
    - not have the correct resources for a task; and
    - appear to always be in the 'here and now'.

Chapter 5
TASK INITIATION

What is it?

This one is short and sweet: task initiation is the executive functioning skill of being able to start a task or activity on time and efficiently. It essentially means the ability to begin a task without procrastination or hesitation. Task initiation is an important part of managing day-to-day tasks and achieving goals.

Task initiation and classroom success

Have you ever had that child who never seems to start their work? I can think of one learner from my first-ever class who always sat staring into space at the start of a writing task. Other learners would have written whole paragraphs before he put pencil to paper. Despite me providing a modelled text, a writing frame and a sentence starter or two, this learner always claimed that he was thinking about what to write. Just as I would reach frustration point, he would then find the longest possible route to walk around the classroom to get to the bin to sharpen his pencil very, very slowly before taking the scenic route back to his seat.

As a result, my learner often produced very little work, meaning that it was difficult to assess what he had learned in each lesson. It also meant that he required lots of adult support at the start of each task to begin.

Looking back, I now recognise that this learner may well have had a particular difficulty with the executive functioning skill of task initiation. It was not necessarily the fact that he would not start – more that he could not start.

DOI: 10.4324/9781003534075-5

Learners who find task initiation difficult might:

- experience difficulties with starting tasks independently;
- display work avoidance behaviours;
- have difficulties with initiating conversations;
- be happy for others to take the lead;
- appear to be unfocused;
- start a task independently but take a long time to do so;
- spend a long time observing what others are doing before beginning a task; and
- seek immediate support before trialling independently.

Let us bring these difficulties to life with a case study: meet Layla.

Task initiation in the classroom – a case study

Background information

It is difficult to truly assess Layla's level of skills, knowledge and understanding in a written format, as she never manages to complete a written assessment. This is because she just never seems to 'get going' independently. If left to her own devices, by the time she has started, it is time to stop working.

Layla has received support via her school's graduated response to special educational needs for two terms. This support has focused on the area of cognition and learning – working to build her independence and self-help skills in the classroom.

Information from the class teacher

Layla has access to scaffolds designed to promote independent working. These work well for a while, but not necessarily consistently. Her response depends on the complexity of the task. If Layla perceives that the task is too difficult, she appears to instantly give up and does not even attempt to make a start. The class teaching assistant often steps in to support her in starting tasks.

Observations

English: writing a non-chronological report about Greece

Layla sat with her class on the carpet watching the class teacher model how to start the report. The class teaching assistant sat close to her offering additional explanation and recording the process as a drawn 'to-do' list on a mini whiteboard. Once the demonstration was complete, Layla returned to her table with the 'to-do' list. She sat looking back through the pages of her workbook. After five minutes, the teaching assistant gave her a sentence starter to build on. Layla said thank you and then sat without picking up her pencil. The teaching assistant went back to Layla after a further five minutes and together they used a voice recording device to record an opening sentence. Layla played this back to herself three times before attempting to write it down.

History: sequencing a timeline

Layla sat quietly during the lesson introduction. She did not contribute to the whole class discussion and allowed her partner to go first and take the lead in any 'think, pair, share' activities. When the class were instructed to cut out the pictures and sequence them to make a timeline, Layla sat twirling the scissors on her fingers. After approximately three minutes, she got up and had a drink of water and stopped off in the book corner to tidy up some of the books. On her way back to her seat, she stopped to look at how other children were completing the task. She then sat down in her seat and began to cut out the pictures. By the time Layla had cut out the pictures, it was time to stop for lunch. Layla had not sequenced them or stuck them into her book.

Support and impact to date

Support	Impact
Provision of sentence starters to begin all writing tasks.	With an adult prompt, Layla will use the sentence starter. She can add one idea which she usually records but then stops the task until an adult supports her to follow the same process with a sentence starter to write each subsequent sentence.
Use of a sand timer with the expectation that Layla starts the task before the sand timer runs out.	This has had no real impact. Even with the threat of lost breaktime, Layla struggles to begin a task.
A peer buddy to model how to start.	This has worked well, as Layla will copy what they do.

Next steps It is appropriate to further explore Layla's understanding of what she is asked to do and her understanding in general. This will be important in determining whether she is unable to do the work and thus requires further support and scaffolds or is choosing not to.

To test whether Layla's difficulties with task initiation are either a choice or a genuine need, it is important to put support in place and then evaluate the impact. The following is a toolkit of strategies and approaches that may help.

Task initiation toolkit

Classroom challenges

- Have difficulties with starting tasks independently;
- Display work avoidance behaviours;
- Have difficulties with initiating conversations;
- Are happy for others to take the lead;
- Can appear to be unfocused;
- Start a task independently but take a long time to do so;
- Spend a long time observing what others are doing before beginning a task; and
- Seek immediate support before trialling independently.

Tools

1 Provide a ready to work checklist so that the learner knows exactly what they should have in place ready to start the task. This will help them to avoid prolonged procrastination. You can add a layer of challenge by giving a time limit to complete the checklist in – for example:

> **Are you ready to work?**
>
>
> - Sitting at my desk
> - Pen and ruler
> - Workbook open on the correct page
> - Date written
> - Title written
> - Comfy in my chair
>
> Image designed by Freepik

2 Offer sentence starters. The learner can then build on the suggested start.

3 Record whole class instructions using a voice recording device and give this to the learner. They can then play back the instructions as many times as they require to help them remember what to do and how to get started.

4 Give a clear role/purpose in group work. Provide a brief checklist of what that role looks like/involves.

5 Establish and rehearse consistent routines for beginning a task to make the process become more automatic.

6 Provide support for transitions between tasks using a 'now and next' board. This will help the learner to know what they should be doing now and what is expected of them next. Further stages can be added, such as first, next, then – for example:

Now	Next
Writing	Maths

7 Provide a peer study buddy to model how to start the task.

8 Take an 'I do, we do, you do' approach so that the task is gradually handed over to the learner to reduce overwhelm.

9 Begin tasks with a short success-driven activity to build the learner's confidence. This will breed a 'feelgood' factor which will encourage the learner to continue with greater independence and focus.

Images by Freepik

REFLECTION POINT

- Which tool from the toolkit do you think would be the most helpful for a learner that you have identified as having difficulties with task initiation?
- Why do you think this tool would be the most effective choice?

Here are five top tips which you can share with a colleague that could be effective in supporting learners with task initiation difficulties. These top tips could pair well with selected tools from the planning and prioritising toolkit:

	Task initiation – five top tips
	Be curious – avoid assuming that the learner is choosing not to do the task. There could be a number of reasons why they are finding it difficult to get started. It is important to rule out factors such as lack of understanding, feeling overwhelmed or perceiving that they do not have the right tools for the job.
	Aim for gradual handover of a task by taking an 'I do, we, do, you do' approach. This will build confidence and avoid overwhelm.
	Develop consistent and embedded routines for beginning tasks with accompanying visual support. This will help to develop an automatic approach from the learner.
	Use written or drawn checklists/to-do lists to support learners in knowing exactly what to do when. Teach the learner to develop these independently.
	Offer supportive scaffolds such as writing frames, sentence starters and visual cues to aid the initial part of thinking about the task.

Images by Freepik

To support parents and caregivers who may have concerns about their child's task initiation skills, the following is something that you can share:

Task initiation – a quick guide

What is it?

Task initiation is the executive functioning skill of being able to start a task or activity on time and efficiently. It essentially means the ability to begin a task without procrastination or hesitation. Task initiation is an important part of managing day-to-day tasks and achieving goals.

Children who find it hard to initiate a task might:

- have difficulties with starting tasks independently;
- display work avoidance behaviours;
- have difficulties with initiating conversations;
- be happy for others to take the lead;
- appear to be unfocused;
- start a task independently but take a long time to do so;
- spend a long time observing what others are doing before beginning a task; and
- seek immediate support before trialling independently.

How can you support your child to develop task initiation skills?

1. Try to avoid assuming that your child is choosing not to start a task. Consider carefully whether they might be finding the task overwhelming or perceive that it is too challenging for them to tackle.
2. Spread the load by taking an 'I do, we do, you do' approach. This will build their confidence and make them feel supported.
3. Think about one small thing that you can do to help them get started, such as giving them the start of a sentence to complete.
4. Provide a checklist of all the things that they will need to start a task.
5. Have a race – see whether your child can beat you to start the task. Award points or a small prize if they succeed. Making it fun takes away a lot of the stress and anxiety related to getting started.

Images by Freepik

Finally, here are three supportive activities which can be used to support your learners to develop their task initiation skills:

Task initiation – skill builders

The following activities are all designed to help your learner to develop their task initiation skills. When completing these activities, it is important to draw specific attention to:

- the skill that they are using;
- why it works; and
- how the skill can be transferred back to the classroom.

Ready, steady, go!	Have a race! Who will be the first to start the task? Award points or a small prize for the winner. It is important to remember that the learner will need to succeed with this approach to encourage them and to build their confidence.
I, we, you	Choose a task that the learner is good at. It could be something that they find highly personally motivating. Ask the learner to model the task while you watch. Repeat the process but begin the task together, allowing the learner to be the teacher. Finally, attempt the task with the learner watching and giving you feedback. This will develop their confidence in beginning tasks as they take on the mantle of expert.
Now and next	Ask the learner to make their own 'now and next' board, considering carefully what they must do right now to start the task and what to do next.

Images by Freepik

Let's revisit Layla. Following the last round of support detailed in her case study, further assessment took place to explore whether her difficulties were a case of could not start or would not start. The assessments revealed that Layla's receptive language levels were not in line with her chronological age and that, in general, she was finding it hard to understand what to do and feeling a little overwhelmed. This caused her to worry and forget crucial task instructions. This led to the following support shown in Table 5.1:

TABLE 5.1 Layla's revised provision

Support	Impact	Suggested next step
Use of a voice recording device. The teacher recorded instructions as she gave them to the class using the voice recording device. When it was time to start, the device was given to Layla so that she could play back the instructions as many times as she needed.	This worked well. Layla played back the instructions as and when needed and was able to start more of her tasks with independence.	Encourage Layla to task responsibility for recording the instructions herself to further develop her independence.
Provision of a 'ready to work' checklist.	Layla responded well to this. With lots of rehearsal, she was able to develop automaticity by following a consistent task-starting routine.	Begin to withdraw the prompt card to see whether Layla can follow the routine without the prompt.

CHAPTER TAKEAWAYS

- Task initiation is the executive functioning skill of being able to start a task or activity on time and efficiently. It essentially means the ability to begin a task without procrastination or hesitation. Task initiation is an important part of managing day-to-day tasks and achieving goals.
- It is important to avoid assuming that the learner is choosing not to do the task. There could be a number of reasons why they are finding it difficult to get started. Therefore, it is important to rule out factors such as lack of understanding, feeling overwhelmed or perceiving that they do not have the right tools for the job.
- Learners who experience difficulties with task initiation might:
  - experience difficulties with starting tasks independently;
  - display work avoidance behaviours;
  - have difficulties with initiating conversations;
  - be happy for others to take the lead;
  - appear to be unfocused;
  - start a task independently but take a long time to do so;
  - spend a long time observing what others are doing before beginning a task; and
  - seek immediate support before trialling independently.
- Make sure your learner perceives that they have the tools and support that they need to tackle the task. This avoids procrastination and feelings of overwhelm and helplessness. The development of consistent, well-embedded routines for beginning tasks with accompanying visual support can be a simple but effective way of helping.

Chapter 6
ORGANISATION

What is it?

When we consider organisation as part of executive functioning, we refer to two distinct things. The first is the ability to organise your approach to a task. This links closely to the planning and prioritising and task initiation skills we explored earlier. Within this is the ability to manage time, choose the right resources at the right time, plan what to do and when to do it, keep track of where you are towards task completion and potentially multitask. The second element relates to organising your workspace so that the physical environment is conducive to efficient working practices.

Having sound organisational skills has a big impact on our success in our professional and personal lives. Without these skills, a lot can go wrong – we would never make it on time to appointments, meet work deadlines, get out of the house on time or cook a meal.

> **REFLECTION POINT**
>
> Can you think of an element of your day-to-day working practices or personal life in which having strong organisational skills is necessary?

Organisation and classroom success

Let's imagine that you have tasked your class with designing and making healthy sandwiches for the class next door. There are several components to this task that will need organising.

If the organisation of this task is not effective the whole thing could go wrong.

DOI: 10.4324/9781003534075-6

TABLE 6.1 Sandwich-making task stages

Before making the sandwich
• Researching what constitutes a health sandwich.
• Finding out what types of sandwiches the learners in the class next door do and do not like.
• Finding out whether any of the learners from the class next door have food allergies or intolerances.
• Deciding what kinds of sandwiches to make.
• Deciding on quantities of ingredients.
• Writing a shopping list.
• Shopping for the ingredients.
• Decide who will do what when the task is started.
Making the sandwiches
• Setting up and maintaining the workspace so that it is conducive to efficient working practices.
• Buttering the bread.
• Filling the sandwiches.
• Cutting them into triangles.
• Reprioritising and changing tasks if needed.
• Managing time.
After making the sandwiches
• Placing them in sandwich bags and labelling them with the ingredients.
• Cleaning up the workspace.
• Delivering the sandwiches to the class next door.
• Evaluating the success of the task.

REFLECTION POINT

- Think of a learner who has difficulties with organisation. How would their organisation skills impact on their ability to complete the sandwich task?

Organisation skills do not just apply to classroom learning situations. They are also essential in allowing our learners to access wider school life and the world beyond school. Here are some examples of things that our learners need to be well organised for:

- communicating with their families about things such as after-school events and school trips so that the school receives consent and payment;
- having the right equipment in their school bag for the right day;
- completing homework tasks and handing them in on time;
- ordering lunch or break time snacks; and
- arriving on time.

Being able to do these things impacts on classroom success and eventual employability. Learners who experience challenges with developing organisational skills might:

- experience difficulties with time management;
- appear to be forgetful of things such as PE kit, homework and specific lesson resources;
- find it difficult to select the right resources for a task;
- get lost in tasks easily, so work produced is often disorganised;
- miss deadlines;
- often leave things until the last minute;
- appear to be untidy;
- lose things easily;
- have difficulties with sequencing;
- find it challenging to follow a sequence of steps in a task or the stages in multi-step instructions; and
- get muddled easily.

Let's explore what these difficulties can look like in more depth with a case study.

Organisation – a case study
Background information
Nadim is working above age-related expectations in most areas of the curriculum. He has a sound understanding of concepts and appears to really enjoy learning. However, Nadim experiences lots of difficulties with presenting his work in an organised and cohesive way. This is also the case when he shares his ideas verbally. His contributions show excellent knowledge and understanding but often lack a logical order.
An assessment from a speech and language therapist has revealed that Nadim does not have a notable difficulty with expressive language in the main but there are mild difficulties relating to sequencing and grammar.
Information from the class teacher
Nadim works well in class. He is enthusiastic and has a lovely sense of humour. Nadim often loses things and his workspace is never tidy. He often has the wrong equipment for lessons and is usually late.
Nadim's work is full of great ideas and reflects sound knowledge and understanding of concepts but is often muddled. His mind appears to work like the ball in a pinball machine – pinging everywhere at pace!
Observations
Design technology: making a pillowcase from his own design
Nadim's design was ambitious and detailed. He had previously produced a well-thought-out design that met the brief and was carefully labelled. When it was time to start making the pillowcase, Nadim found it difficult to gather the resources he needed. He kept having to stop work and fetch something that he had forgotten from the resource station. Nadim frequently observed the process that his peers were following and tried hard to match his own work to this. This was supportive but not necessarily the right approach for what he aimed to achieve. Nadim's workspace became very untidy very quickly. This meant that he was unable to find the fastenings he intended to use. He also sewed up all four edges of the pillowcase without putting in the stuffing. This meant that he had to unpick one edge. Due to this, Nadim did not finish making his pillowcase in the allotted time.

Transition from maths to outdoor breaktime

Nadim placed his maths book in the middle of the table as requested but left his pencil and ruler inside it. He joined the line to go to the cloakroom. Once in the cloakroom, Nadim needed to seek support to be able to find his coat. Once he had his coat on, he went out to the playground. Five minutes later, he returned to the classroom to collect his fruit and drink, which he had unfortunately forgotten.

Support and impact to date

Support	Impact
Resource checklists to help Nadim gather the right equipment for the right lesson.	These work well, provided that he does not lose them!
A visual task timeline is provided as part of a task-slicing approach to support Nadim in knowing what he needs to do and in what order.	Nadim can follow this well but struggles with managing time to get to the end of the timeline. At present, an adult needs to support him to create this resource, as he can miss out stages.
We frequently contact Nadim's parents to ensure that they know about school trips, swimming, after-school events and special assemblies.	This works well, as his parents are very proactive and supportive, but we recognise that Nadim needs supporting to develop the skills to do this independently – particularly with the transition to secondary school on the horizon.

Next steps It is appropriate to review what is in place for Nadim to ensure that he can develop independent organisational skills for the future. His disorganised writing also needs to be developed so that we can see the true extent of his knowledge and understanding.

There are lots of options available to support Nadim in developing his organisational skills. The following toolkit shows many ways in which this can be done.

Organisation toolkit

Classroom challenges

- Experience difficulties with time management;
- Appear to be forgetful of things such as PE kit, homework and specific lesson resources;
- Find it difficult to select the right resources for a task;
- Get lost in tasks easily, so work produced is often disorganised;
- Miss deadlines;
- Often leave things until the last minute;
- Appear to be untidy;
- Lose things easily;
- Have difficulties with sequencing;
- Find it challenging to follow a sequence of steps in a task or the stages in multi-step instructions; and
- Become muddled easily.

Tools

1   Offer a highly visual timer to support time management. Sand timers, time tamer clocks or digital devices are all effective, in that learners can see the time ticking down and specific times can be set to match the time required for a task. Some timers offer the bonus of a traffic-light system which can be matched to specific times so that learners knows when the time is halfway through or can match the task to the colour shown. This is a helpful strategy but not for all, as some learners can find that a timer adds a layer of stress.

2   Use of resource checklists that are specific to events and/or lessons. These can include a written list, a visual aid using cartoons or photographs of concrete objects for the learner to match their resources to. For things such as PE kits, it is helpful if the visual aid shows the learner their personal items.

3   Colour code and simplify the learner's timetable. You might like to focus on one day at a time and colour code when they will need to bring in something specific from home, such as their PE kit.

4   In line with your school's electronic device policy, teach the learner to set phone reminders linked to when things such as reading books, homework, musical instruments and PE kits need to be brought into school. Special events such as special assemblies, trips and visiting theatre companies can also be added to this.

5   Have one central place for the learner to store their belongings. It can often be helpful if this is 'the one on the end' (like the last coat peg or tray), so that they can find things more easily. It can also be helpful if this is in a less busy space, to aid their focus when finding things.

6   Carabiner clips can be used to attach additional bags – such as a PE bag – to the learner's main school bag, to limit the number of items that they need to remember to take with them.

7   Colour code equipment according to which subject it relates to. This could include the learner's workbooks.

8   Offer writing frames, flow charts and graphic organisers to help with planning written work.

9   Rehearse sequencing everyday familiar events. This could include using photographs or written statements to order.

10 Make a personal resource placemat for the learner to have on their desk which shows them where everything goes. This will aid them in having a tidy workspace.

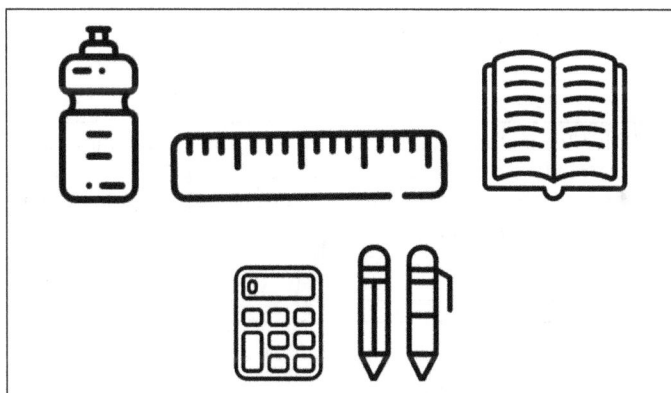

11 Give the learner a voice recording device to record multi-step or complex instructions.

12 Rehearse task slicing. Work with the learner to break large tasks into small manageable steps with a specific time allotted to each task. Create a visual timeline to support this.

Images by Freepik

REFLECTION POINT

- Think back to the sandwich-making task. Which tools from the organisation toolkit might help a learner with organisation difficulties to succeed at this task?

Here are five top tips that you can share with your colleagues to support learners in developing their organisational skills:

	Organisation – five top tips
	Help the learner to stay focused by ensuring that their workspace is tidy and clutter free. Offer a central space where they can store all of their belongings and resources. It is helpful if this is in a quieter and easily accessible area in the classroom.
	Support the learner to develop their sequencing skills. Start by ordering the steps in familiar everyday events, such as getting dressed. Develop this to sequencing what needs to be done to complete a small project or classroom task. Develop visual prompts to support this process.
	Use highly visual timers that show learners time passing. This will help them to know exactly how long they have left to complete a task.
	Use written or drawn checklists/to-do lists to support learners in knowing exactly what to do and when. Teach the learner to develop these independently as part of a task-slicing approach.
	Utilise technology. Voice notes, an electronic calendar and scheduled reminders can all be really helpful. Teach the learner how to use these tools independently and to match what they need to put into their device to their school timetable.

Images by Freepik

For parents and caregivers who may have concerns about their child's task organisation skills, here is something that you can share:

Organisation – a quick guide

What is it?

'Organisation' refers to two distinct things. The first is the ability to organise your approach to a task. Within this is the ability to manage time, choose the right resources at the right time, plan what to do and when to do it, keep track of where you are towards task completion and potentially multitask. The second element relates to organising your workspace so that the physical environment is conducive to efficient working practices.

Children who find the skill of being organised challenging might:

- experience difficulties with time management;

- appear to be forgetful of things such as PE kit, homework and specific lesson resources;

- find it difficult to select the right resources for a task;

- get lost in tasks easily, so work produced is often disorganised;

- miss deadlines;

- often leave things until the last minute;

- appear to be untidy;

- lose things easily;

- have difficulties with sequencing;

- find it challenging to follow a sequence of steps in a task or the stages in multi-step instructions; and

- become muddled easily.

How can you support your child to develop their organisation skills?

1. Teach them to use the reminder function and calendar on their tablet or phone. You can add in reminders for things such as when their PE kit is needed in school or when they have a homework deadline to meet or after-school club to attend.
2. Practise sequencing everyday events such as getting dressed and ready for school. Once they can do this quickly and effectively, explore sequencing bigger projects, such as how to approach a homework assignment.
3. Use a voice recording device such as voice notes on their phone to record important things that they need to remember, such as messages or complex instructions. They can play these back as many times as required.
4. Create a checklist of the items that they need to have in their school bag each day.
5. Create activity flowcharts which show what needs to be done and in what order.

Images by Freepik

To finish, here are three supportive skill builder activities which can be used to support your learners to develop their task initiation skills.

Organisation – skill builders

The following activities are all designed to help your learner to develop their task initiation skills. When completing these activities, it is important to draw specific attention to:

- the skill that they are using;

- why it works; and

- how the skill can be transferred back to the classroom.

Tidy space, tidy mind	Encourage your learner to take responsibility for a specific area of the classroom. It is their job to organise this space and keep it tidy. Allow them to help you set up a storage system and organise their own resources.
Checkmate!	Give your learner responsibility for creating resource checklists that the whole class can use. These might be: • what should be in your PE bag; • what is needed for maths; or • a ready to work checklist. Encourage them to model for others how these should be used.
Frame it!	Show the learner how to use a writing frame to order their ideas and plan a piece of writing.

Images by Freepik

It is now time to revisit Nadim from our case study. His support moved on to focus on developing independence in using the strategies designed to develop his organisation skills.

TABLE 6.2 Nadim's revised provision

Support	Impact	Suggested next step
Nadim was supported to create resource checklists for the whole class and to model how to use them.	Nadim will independently use the resource checklists that he developed. He feels a sense of ownership over them and takes pride in others feeling helped by what he has designed.	Start to wean the checklists away so that Nadim has opportunities to recall and be organised without them.
Use of the reminder and calendar function on his tablet.	Nadim is confident in populating the calendar and reminders himself. School no longer contacts his parents as often, as his device aids him in remembering what is needed when and what special events are coming up.	Continue with this tool so that it is thoroughly embedded.
Use of writing frames and flow charts to help Nadim plan his work using a coherent structure.	The use of writing frames and flow charts has helped Nadim to structure his writing much more effectively. This makes his message much easier to understand.	Increase the complexity of the writing frames and flow charts to further develop the structure of his writing.

CHAPTER TAKEAWAYS

- 'Organisation' refers to two distinct things. The first is the ability to organise your approach to a task. Within this is the ability to manage time, choose the right resources at the right time, plan what to do and when to do it, keep track of where you are towards task completion and potentially multitask. The second element relates to organising your workspace so that the physical environment is conducive to efficient working practices.
- Children who find being organised challenging might:
  - experience difficulties with time management;
  - appear to be forgetful of things such as PE kit, homework and specific lesson resources;
  - find it difficult to select the right resources for a task;
  - get lost in tasks easily, so work produced is often disorganised;
  - miss deadlines;
  - often leave things until the last minute;
  - appear to be untidy;
  - lose things easily;
  - have difficulties with sequencing;
  - find it challenging to follow a sequence of steps in a task or the stages in multi-step instructions;
  - become muddled easily.
- When supporting learners to develop their organisation skills, it is important not only to focus on their task organisation skills, but also to consider how to help them to organise their physical workspace.

Chapter 7
IMPULSE CONTROL

What is it?

'Impulse control' refers to our ability to consider the outcome and consequences of our future actions before we proceed. This involves resisting our instant urges. This skill acts as a self-control mechanism that is part of a wider suite of cognitive skills that we use to manage our behaviour and decision making.

To illustrate impulse control, we can consider the famous marshmallow experiment carried out in the 1960s by psychologist Walter Mischel at Stanford University (Mischel & Ebbesen 1970). The experiment measured self-control, or how well a child can inhibit impulsive behaviours and work towards longer-term goals – what is termed 'delayed gratification'. Participating children were offered a choice between having one marshmallow immediately or receiving two marshmallows if they opted to wait. Arguably, the actual findings related to impulse control are not the interesting thing here, but rather the findings of Mischel's follow-up studies.

In the 1990s, Mischel revisited the same children from the original marshmallow experiment to explore how they were doing as adults (Shoda, Mischel & Peake 1990). He found that the children who had waited longer to receive their marshmallow treats in his original experiment had achieved greater overall success in their school assessment scores, better health (measured by body mass index) and better attainments in higher education. Furthermore, the parents and caregivers of the children who had waited longer for their marshmallows were found to be more likely to say that those children planned well for the future and handled stress effectively.

This shows the importance of supporting our learners to develop effective impulse control skills as part of our approach to developing sound overall executive functioning.

DOI: 10.4324/9781003534075-7

There are two types of impulsivity that we should be aware of in the classroom: trait impulsivity and state impulsivity. 'Trait impulsivity' refers to a relatively stable personality characteristic where someone has a general tendency to act without thinking or considering the consequences. This can be described as a long-term predisposition. 'State impulsivity' describes a temporary, in-the-moment increase in impulsive behaviour which is activated by specific environmental factors or emotional states. This means that it can alter depending on the situation.

REFLECTION POINT

- Would you say that you experience state impulsivity or trait impulsivity?
- Why is this and what does it look like for you?

Impulse control and classroom success

Let's think about those learners who experience difficulties with impulse control. In your classroom, you might see that these learners:

- 'dive in' to tasks and situations, appearing not to think before acting;
- do not link consequences to actions;
- are easily distracted;
- distract others;
- have difficulties with following instructions;
- appear not to think of others before acting;
- call out answers;
- have difficulties with turn taking;
- find it hard to wait;
- share information, needs and/or wants immediately;
- find it challenging to follow rules in games/shared tasks with peers;
- have difficulties with seeing a task through to the end;
- have difficulties with sharing;
- experience quick changes in emotions;
- focus on the end goal/outcome; and
- can seek instant gratification.

REFLECTION POINT

- Can you think of a learner who has difficulties managing their impulse control?
- What does their behaviour look like in the classroom?

Often, learners who experience some form of difficulty with impulsivity can find themselves getting into trouble when their actions did not come from a place of malice. It literally can be that they got 'caught up in the moment' and dived in without thinking. If this continues long term, it can have an impact on their self-esteem and overall wellbeing. Consider the child who is constantly reprimanded for not waiting, calling out and upsetting others because they appeared selfish when they did not stop to consider others. They could potentially be in a permanent state of anxiety about where their next telling off is coming from. This could ultimately impact negatively on their chances of achieving classroom success.

Let's explore what these difficulties can look like in more depth with a case study – meet Lewis.

Impulse control – a case study

Background information

Lewis has lots of energy. His family report that he does not seem to stop and is 'always on the go'.

Over time, Lewis has received several sanctions for his actions in school. These have included:

- low-level disruptive behaviours such as calling out and fiddling with resources;

- hurting others because he has pushed them out of the way to get a resource or toy that he would like; and

- friendship disputes where he has hurt others because he wanted his turn first.

The usual reward charts and incentives have proved to be unsuccessful in supporting Lewis to manage his behaviour.

Information from the class teacher

Lewis can be such a lovely young man. He can be very kind and caring towards his peers. Unfortunately, he also can hurt others because he needs to act upon a particular outcome that he has in mind immediately.

When something has gone wrong, Lewis is very remorseful. He is usually upset because he has unintentionally upset others and once he has been supported to reflect upon a scenario, he is quick to apologise.

Observations

Playtime

Lewis clearly enjoys the opportunities to be physical that playtime presents. Once outside, he ran around the perimeter of the playground. As soon as a peer came out with a football, he ran straight over and kicked the ball as hard as he could. Unfortunately, this resulted in the ball going over the fence into a neighbour's garden. Lewis' friends were understandably cross about this. Lewis ran away from them and began chasing a learner from his class. It appeared that he had wanted to join a game of tag but had not asked to do so.

Art: creating a collage

The children were presented with a range of old magazines, comics, catalogues and leaflets that they could use to create a collage. Lewis had decided that he wanted to create a football-themed collage and, from his seat, identified three magazines that he wanted. When instructed to fetch the resources, Lewis jumped up quickly, ran across the room and pushed two other children out of the way to get to the magazines. When seated at his table, he cut out the images that he wanted and put the remaining magazines in the bin. His teacher spoke to him to explain that other children may have wanted some of the images from the magazines that he had put in the bin. Lewis explained that he was sorry and had not thought to ask whether anyone else needed them.

Support and impact to date	
Support	**Impact**
Visual task timelines aimed at supporting Lewis to see the many steps required to be completed to progress to the end of a task.	These work well when Lewis is encouraged to use them. However, if a task is highly personally motivating, he will skip straight to the end. This means that he misses crucial mid-stage learning opportunities and that his work is incomplete.
Turn-taking games in which Lewis must wait for his go.	Lewis can take turns in a structured and adult-led situation. However, he does not transfer this to independent play situations, especially in the playground.
Cause and effect exploration taking the form of a debrief following a difficult situation in which Lewis is supported to identify what went wrong, who was affected and how the situation might better be approached in future.	Lewis is good at reflecting on what has happened. He is usually honest and remorseful. However, he does not consistently apply the lesson from considering how to better approach the situation in future.

Next steps

It is important that the approaches deployed to support Lewis are reviewed and adapted as only minor impact can be seen, particularly in terms of his application of taught strategies.

The good news is that there are lots of tools available to support learners similar to Lewis in developing their impulse control skills.

Impulse control toolkit

Classroom challenges

- 'Dive in' to tasks and situations, appearing not to think before acting;
- Do not link consequences to actions;
- Are easily distracted;
- Distract others;
- Have difficulties with following instructions;
- Appear to not think of others before acting;
- Call out answers;
- Have difficulties with turn taking;
- Find it hard to wait;
- Share information, needs and/or wants immediately;
- Find it challenging to follow rules in games/shared tasks with peers;
- Have difficulties with seeing a task through to the end;
- Have difficulties with sharing;
- Experience quick changes in emotions;
- Focus on the end goal/outcome; and
- Can seek instant gratification.

Tools
1 Offer activities which focus on linking cause and effect. For very young children, playing with cause and effect toys could be an appropriate starting point. For older children, you may wish to explore specific scenarios posing 'What if?' questions.
2 When exploring the solution to a problem, list all available solutions – even the ones that seem crazy! Work through each of them, determining which ones are positive solutions and which are less so.
3 Wonder aloud to show your learner how you decide on an outcome. This makes the invisible process of decision making visible and gives the learner a valuable model to use themselves.
4 Practise waiting using burst-pause games. These games are a way to build anticipation and engagement by pausing after an action or noise. Games based around 'ready, steady, go' commands, musical statues and those involving countdowns before action are perfect.
5 Provide learners who call out answers or ideas with a mini-whiteboard and dry wipe pen. They can then always answer or contribute using this tool rather than calling out.
6 Play structured turn-taking games. Initially, these may need to be adult led. Gradually, a play partner and then more peers can be introduced.
7 Play games that involve an unpredictable outcome, such as Buckaroo, Pop Up Pirates and Kerplunk!
8 Have a 'park it' system. This could be a deck of Post-it notes on which the learner can write their immediate thoughts, needs, wishes and wants. Once these have been recorded, the Post-it note can be 'parked' for later discussion with an adult at a mutually agreed time.
9 Use a comic strip conversation approach to 'unpick' situations in which feelings, thoughts and behaviours need to be explored. Comic strip conversations were created by Carol Gray in 1994. They are simple visual representations of conversation/scenarios that can show the things that are actually said in a conversation, how people might be feeling and what people's intentions might be (Gray 1994). This will help the learner to consider the consequences of their actions.
10 Use social stories to explore how to respond in situations where decisions need to be made. Rehearse the actions from the story to allow automaticity to develop.
11 Work to complete tasks which will take a long time to finish – ideally, these should be tasks that will need to be paused and revisited to continue. These could include craft projects or building complex models using construction toys.

Here are five top tips to support learners in developing their impulse control skills. They can be shared with your colleagues to support their learners too:

STOP!	**Impulse control – five top tips**

	Be professionally curious. It is important not to assume that learners who demonstrate difficulties with impulse control are being malicious or 'naughty'. It is essential to explore what the underlying causes might be. What is the learner anticipating?
	Rehearse the skill of waiting but be explicit about what you are doing and why. This will make the learner aware of the skill that they are developing and when it is important for them to use it.
	Work on cause and effect. 'What might happen if?' questions related to real-life scenarios are a good starting point.
	Use written or drawn checklists/to-do lists to support learners in knowing exactly what to do and in what order. This will help them to identify the steps involved to complete a task.
	Use countdowns to help your learner wait before responding.

Images by Freepik

For parents and caregivers who may have concerns about their child's impulsivity, the following is a resource that you can share:

STOP!

Impulse control – a quick guide

What is it?

'Impulse control' refers to our ability to consider the outcome and consequences of our future actions before we proceed. This involves resisting our instant urges. This skill acts as a self-control mechanism that is part of a wider suite of cognitive skills that we use to manage our behaviour and decision making.

Children who find impulse control challenging might:

- 'dive in' to tasks and situations, appearing not to think before acting;
- not link consequences to actions;
- be easily distracted;
- distract others;
- have difficulties with following instructions;
- appear not to think of others before acting;
- call out answers;
- have difficulties with turn taking;
- find it hard to wait;
- share information, needs and/or wants immediately;
- find it challenging to follow rules in games/shared tasks with peers;
- have difficulties with seeing a task through to the end;
- have difficulties with sharing;
- experience quick changes in emotions;
- focus upon the end goal/outcome; and
- seek instant gratification.

How can you support your child to develop their impulse control skills?

- Make waiting fun by playing games which involve countdowns or a 'ready, steady, go' approach before they can act.
- Model your own decision-making progress by thinking aloud – for example: 'I wonder if we should have burgers or salad for tea? I think salad would be best because ...'
- Involve your child in tasks that will need to be completed in several sittings, such as building a complex model using construction toys.

Images by Freepik

To finish, here are three skill builder activities which focus on developing impulse control skills:

	Impulse control – skill builders
The following activities are all designed to help your learner to develop their task initiation skills. When completing these activities, it is important to draw specific attention to: • the skill that they are using; • why it works; and • how the skill can be transferred back to the classroom.	
3, 2, 1 go!	Play games which involve a countdown. The learner is not allowed to act until the countdown is complete. Increase the length of the countdown to encourage waiting for longer periods of time.
It takes time!	Work towards a goal that will take time to achieve. This task should be the sort that will need to be completed in several sittings. Delayed gratification is what you are after. Building complex models using construction toys could be a good starting point.
Tidy up to focus!	Make sure that the learner's space is tidy, calm and uncluttered. This will help them to focus on the task and what is needed to achieve success.

Images by Freepik

Back to Lewis – in Table 7.1, let's see if a new approach has helped.

TABLE 7.1 Lewis's revised provision

Support	Impact	Suggested next step
Lots of games which took the form of a burst-pause approach, with added work on metacognition.	This helped Lewis to become much more aware of the skill he was practising and why it was important for the classroom. He can now be seen to stop and wait.	This now needs consolidating and embedding for consistency.
Continued use of his visual task timeline, but with support for Lewis to co-construct his timeline so that he has ownership of the task.	Lewis really likes having the opportunity to be part of constructing his timeline. This means that he is much more likely to follow it, as he feels a sense of ownership.	Work to achieving handover so that Lewis can construct his timelines independently.
Structured turn taking in real-life playground scenarios.	Lewis is beginning to apply the concept of turn taking in his independent play, as the rehearsal scenarios are real and personally relevant.	Continue to embed and consolidate this approach.

REFLECTION POINT

- Why do you think these tools have been more successful for Lewis than those trialled before?

CHAPTER TAKEAWAYS

- 'Impulse control' refers to our ability to consider the outcome and consequences of our future actions before we proceed. This involves resisting our instant urges. This skill acts as a self-control mechanism that is part of a wider suite of cognitive skills that we use to manage our behaviour and decision-making.
- Children who find the skill of impulse control challenging might:
    - 'dive in' to tasks and situations, appearing not to think before acting;
    - not link consequences to actions;
    - be easily distracted;
    - distract others;
    - have difficulties with following instructions;
    - appear not to think of others before acting;
    - call out answers;
    - have difficulties with turn taking;
    - find it hard to wait;
    - share information, needs and/or wants immediately;
    - find it challenging to follow rules in games/shared tasks with peers;
    - have difficulties with seeing a task through to the end;
    - have difficulties with sharing;
    - experience quick changes in emotions;
    - focus on the end goal/outcome; and
    - seek instant gratification.
- For children who demonstrate difficulties with impulse control, it is important to remain professionally curious. Do not assume that learners who demonstrate difficulties with impulse control are being malicious or 'naughty'. It is essential to explore what the underlying causes might be. What is the learner anticipating?

Chapter 8
EMOTIONAL CONTROL

What is it?

'Emotional control' refers to the cognitive ability to identify, manage and regulate your own emotions, which then allows you to respond appropriately to different situations. It is the ability to control your feelings and reactions to stimuli and links closely to self-monitoring.

When we talk about feeling emotionally regulated in the classroom, we are talking about ensuring that our feelings and emotions are in an optimal state so that we are ready and available for learning. I am sure that you can remember times when you have been too upset or angry to process information or access a social situation. If you translate this into the classroom, the same applies to learning.

Development of emotional control includes an awareness of oneself and self-monitoring skills. The regulation of emotions is critical for cognitive tasks and mental dexterity. When we regulate behaviour, the frontal lobe of our brain is at work, with its impulse control, initiation, self-monitoring and other cognitive skills. Furthermore, emotional skill development includes the ability to self-regulate. These skills mature and develop throughout childhood and into adulthood.

When we consider emotional control, we often instantly assume that it refers to learners who demonstrate their emotions in a 'big' way and often in a way that consists of two extremes. Think about those learners who present as calm and serene one minute and suddenly change to screaming, crying and lashing out the next. This can be a sign of a difficulty with identifying and managing emotions in a proactive sense. However, we also must consider the quieter, perhaps more withdrawn learners who 'bottle up' their emotions, quietly bubbling away until they all get released. They too may be experiencing the same challenges.

DOI: 10.4324/9781003534075-8

Emotional control and classroom success

Emotional control is essential for classroom success and within wider school life. It has its part to play in social interactions, decision making and overall wellbeing.

Let us consider a learner who experiences difficulties with emotional control during a common classroom occurrence: a timed multiplication fact recall test, in which learners must answer ten quickfire multiplication questions using only mental arithmetic methods. For a learner with emotional control difficulties, this could potentially go one of two ways. It might be that the learner has learned the multiplication facts to expert level, so feels proud and pleased with their achievements in the test. However, they might be unable to manage the related feelings and emotions and begin boasting and bragging loudly to their classmates in a manner which becomes socially unacceptable. This can lead to conflict. Alternatively, the learner may be unhappy with their performance on the test and become angry and frustrated. This may lead to an explosive outburst as rage spills over. Just as with the first learner, the response may be judged to be socially unacceptable and again cause conflict. For both learners, their classroom relationships, access to learning and overall wellbeing will have been damaged in some way. Consequently, emotional control can be crucial to classroom success.

It is vital that we all acknowledge and validate the feelings and emotions experienced by our learners. It is also crucial to recognise the importance of supporting each learner to sit with and navigate their feelings and emotions in a safe and healthy way. This is conducive to having positive learning experiences and critical to classroom success.

As stated by researchers Graziano, Reavis, Keane and Calkins (2007): 'Our findings suggest that children who have difficulty regulating their emotions have trouble learning in the classroom and are less productive and accurate when completing assignments.'

REFLECTION POINT

- Can you think of a classroom situation in which having strong emotional control skills might be crucial to success?

Learners who experience challenges with emotional control may:

- find it hard to identify their own emotions;
- experience quick changes in emotions;
- become frustrated easily;
- appear to become overwhelmed;
- appear to react disproportionately to the situation;
- withdraw from situations that they perceive to be difficult;

- have difficulties with anger management;
- be involved in arguments with peers;
- be perceived by others to be argumentative; and
- be perceived by others to be defiant.

REFLECTION POINT

- Can you identify a learner who experiences some or all of these challenges with emotional control?
- What impact does this have on their classroom success?

As with the other areas of executive functioning considered so far, let us explore emotional control in more detail with a case study.

Emotional control – a case study

Background information

Emily has always demonstrated some excessively big reactions, which could be described as disproportionate to the situation. When she was much younger, she was described as a child who had frequent tantrums. Now, school staff recognise that Emily becomes dysregulated quickly and often unpredictably. When dysregulated, Emily will cry, scream and lash out, and will sometimes throw classroom equipment such as pencil pots and books.

An assessment from a speech and language therapist has evidenced that Emily has sound situational understanding but finds identifying gradients of linked emotions such as happy, joyful and ecstatic challenging. She is also not yet able to link how her body feels (her physiology) to her changing state and emotions.

Information from the class teacher

Emily is an able learner who is making sound progress across all areas of the curriculum. However, she is not meeting her true potential – she is capable of so much more. It is felt that the underlying reason for this is because she experiences difficulties with identifying and regulating her own emotions. This can lead to her becoming very distressed in the classroom and in the playground – especially when she is in test situations, when she perceives that she has not got adult support to meet her immediate needs or when something does not follow the plan that she intended. This is causing Emily to become isolated from her peers, as many of them find her behaviour when dysregulated unpredictable and alarming.

Observations

English: weekly spelling test of ten spellings given to the children to learn at home

At the start of the test, Emily wrote down the first two words, apparently with ease. She appeared to struggle with the third word and rubbed it out three times. At this point, her cheeks became red. Emily was still writing down the third word when the teacher called out the fourth word. At this point, Emily called out, 'Wait!' The teacher paused and Emily caught up. On the fifth word, Emily slammed her pencil on the table and started to cry. The class teacher went over to Emily and whispered something to her. Emily responded by pushing her paper off her desk onto the floor and swiping her pencil pot off the desk. Her crying became louder and she abandoned the test.

Geography: completing a map of the United Kingdom by labelling key cities and rivers

Emily made excellent contributions during the lesson introduction. It was clear that she knew the names of several important cities and rivers. The children had the opportunity to work independently to label a map blank map using pages from an atlas to support. Emily had to share an atlas with a partner. This turned into a dispute as Emily and her partner disagreed about which page to look at. Emily responded by snatching the atlas and refusing to let her partner look at it at all.

Support and impact to date	
Support	**Impact**
Emily has weekly meetings with a learning mentor. This time is used to discuss scenarios that Emily has found difficult, explore why this might be and consider alternative ways to deal with them should they arise again.	Emily works well in these sessions. She is honest and gives all the right/expected answers. However, she very rarely puts them into practice away from these sessions.
Emily has a feelings thermometer which she is encouraged to use to show how she is feeling. Adults use this as a 'check-in' mechanism.	The impact of this is minimal. Emily can often show how she is feeling but does not manage her feelings in a pro-social manner.
Emily has mindful colouring activities which she can access when she is dysregulated.	Often, it is too late for Emily to access these as she becomes dysregulated so quickly.

Next steps

Emily continues to experience periods of dysregulation throughout the school day which are often unpredictable and lead to elevated levels of distressed behaviour. Consequently, her provision needs reviewing and alternative approaches are required.

The following toolkit presents suggestions which may support Emily and other learners who experience difficulties with emotional control.

Emotional control toolkit

Classroom challenges
• Find it hard to identify their own emotions;
• Experience quick changes in emotions;
• Become frustrated easily;
• Appear to become overwhelmed;
• Appear to react disproportionately to the situation;
• Withdraw from situations that they perceive to be difficult;
• Have difficulties with anger management;
• Be involved in arguments with peers;
• Be perceived by others to be argumentative; and
• Be perceived by others to be defiant.

Tools

1. Set the tone and share your own feelings. This might feel uncomfortable for some of us, but sharing our own feelings with our learners, modelling the responses and strategies that we use and encouraging them to do the same can have a really positive impact.
2. Rehearse grounding techniques such as deep breathing exercises using bubbles and balloons to aid focus; using the senses to identify things that can be seen, touched, smelled, heard and tasted in the environment; and self-massage routines. These should be deployed in times of calm as well as when a learner is approaching becoming dysregulated.
3. Mark for effort, not outcome.
4. Support for transitions to promote a sense of security. This could include prior warning, a countdown with a visual timer, a 'now and next' board and/or objects of reference.
5. Offera classroom safe space for withdrawal. Ideally, this should be a low-arousal area.
6. Whenbeginning a new learning activity/approach, support the learner to identify existing skills and strengths that they can transfer to the task. Work on developing metacognition skills would support this. This will prevent the learner from feeling overwhelmed and that they cannot access a task.
7. Ensure that lessons contain the appropriate level of challenge and scaffolding supports and include several opportunities for success. Have clear success criteria so that the learner will recognise when they have done well. This could take the form of a checklist for the learner to mark.
8. Develop a place for the learner to note their anxieties so that they can be addressed at an appropriate time.
9. Model and celebrate 'failure' and making mistakes as a way of learning that can lead to positive outcomes.
10. Create a personalised wellbeing box containing items and activities that the learner finds soothing and calming. These might include things such as sensory tools, favourite snacks, family photographs and positive affirmations. This box should be used proactively to support the learner before they become dysregulated.
11. Use a traffic-light system to help the learner grade the relative importance of the things that might cause them to become dysregulated and add regulating strategies to each light.
12. Workon naming the feelings that the learner experiences and linking them to their early warning signs so that they can recognise them and act proactively to avoid dysregulation.
13. Use an emotion coaching approach to support the learner, working through the following steps:

   - Notice and become aware of the learner's emotions.

   - Name the emotions that you think the child is experiencing to help them connect their emotions to their behaviour.

   - Show empathy by putting yourself in the learner's shoes: think about when you felt a similar emotion and try to remember what it felt like.

   - Reflect on what happened and why it happened.

   - Involve the learner in problem solving and learning lessons from the situation to apply in future, guiding and involving the learner in this process.

Here are five top tips to support learners in developing their emotional control skills. These tips can be shared with your colleagues to support their learners too:

	Emotional control – five top tips
	Be professionally curious. It is important not to assume that learners who demonstrate difficulties with emotional control are simply having a tantrum and treat this with a behavioural-based sanction. It is essential to explore what the underlying causes might be. What is the learner trying to tell us?
	Support learners to make connections between how their body feels and the emotion that they are experiencing. This will help them to become more aware of their early warning signs and respond proactively to avoid becoming dysregulated.
	Set the tone and share your own feelings. This might feel uncomfortable to begin with, but sharing our own feelings with our learners, modelling the responses and strategies that we use and encouraging them to do the same can have a really positive impact.
	Provide lots of visuals to help your learners identify how they are feeling. Many learners find it easier to show rather than tell.
	Validate and acknowledge all of the emotions that your learners experience but be clear on supporting and expecting your learners to experience them in a safe and healthy way.

Images by Freepik

For parents and caregivers who may have concerns about their child's impulsivity, the following is a resource that you can share:

Emotional control – a quick guide

What is it?

'Emotional control' refers to the ability to identify, manage and regulate your own emotions, which then allows you to respond appropriately to different situations. It is the ability to control your feelings and reactions to stimuli and links closely to self-monitoring. When we talk about feeling emotionally regulated in the classroom, we are making reference to having feelings and emotions that are in an optimal state so that we are ready and available for learning.

Children who find emotional control challenging might:

- find it hard to identify their own emotions;
- experience quick changes in emotions;
- become frustrated easily;
- appear to become overwhelmed;
- appear to react disproportionately to the situation;
- withdraw from situations that they perceive to be difficult;
- have difficulties with anger management;
- be involved in arguments with peers;
- be perceived by others to be argumentative; and
- be perceived by others to be defiant.

How can you support your child to develop their emotional control skills?

- Set the tone and share your own feelings. This might feel uncomfortable for some, but sharing our own feelings with our children, modelling the responses and strategies that we use and encouraging them to do the same can have a really positive impact.
- Work on naming the feelings that your child experiences and linking them to their early warning signs so that they can recognise them and act proactively to avoid dysregulation.
- Model and celebrate 'failure' and making mistakes in day-to-day tasks as a way of learning that can lead to positive outcomes.
- Validate and acknowledge the emotions that your child experiences but establish clear expectations and strategies for dealing with them in a safe and healthy way.

Images by Freepik

To finish, here are three skill builder activities which focus on developing emotional control skills:

Emotion control – skill builders

The following activities are all designed to help your learner to develop their emotional control skills. When completing these activities, it is important to draw specific attention to:

- the skill that they are using;
- why it works; and
- how the skill can be transferred back to the classroom.

Depersonalise	Some learners will find it hard to talk about their own emotions. To begin with, it might be more helpful to explore the emotions of characters in films, books and comics. Your learners may also benefit from using puppets or soft toys to roleplay scenarios and explore the emotions linked to these.
Be mindful	Being mindful involves being aware and present in the moment, without judgement. Offer short, focused activities such as colouring, breathwork and using the senses to connect with the environment to soothe and calm. This should be done proactively, before the learner becomes dysregulated.
Connect!	Make connections between how your learner's body feels and the emotions that they are experiencing. Play 'Guess the emotion'. Can your learner guess the emotion from the description of how the body feels?

Images by Freepik

It is now time to revisit Emily to look at the impact of the new support that she has been offered.

TABLE 8.1 Emily's revised provision

Support	Impact	Suggested next step
Emotion coaching.	This has been successful as it takes place 'in the moment', meaning that Emily has been able to connect her emotions directly to a situation and participate in a problem-solving and planning approach at the time. This has meant that learning is 'live'.	Continue with this approach, allowing Emily increased opportunities to lead the problem-solving and planning part of the process.
Praising and marking for effort, not outcome.	Emily is much happier when we focus on her positive dispositions and attitudes. This has made her try harder to show these in class.	Continue with this approach and encourage Emily to identify these within herself.
Use of a personalised wellbeing box.	Emily loves her box. As it is personal to her, she is much more willing to engage and is becoming more proactive in accessing it before she becomes dysregulated.	Continue with this approach, allowing Emily to refresh the contents of her box as needed.

REFLECTION POINT

- Are there any other tools that you think could work well for Emily?
- Why have you chosen these?

CHAPTER TAKEAWAYS

- 'Emotional control' refers to the ability to identify, manage and regulate your own emotions, which then allows you to make appropriate responses to different situations. It is the ability to control your feelings and reactions to stimuli and links closely with self-monitoring.
- Children who find the skill of impulse control challenging might:
    - find it hard to identify their own emotions;
    - exhibit emotions that can change very quickly;
    - become frustrated easily;
    - appear to become overwhelmed;
    - appear to react disproportionately to the situation;
    - withdraw from situations that they perceive to be difficult;
    - have difficulties with anger management;
    - be involved in arguments with peers;
    - be perceived by others to be argumentative; and
    - be perceived by others to be defiant.
- For learners who experience challenges with emotional control, it is important to remain professionally curious. We should not assume that learners who demonstrate difficulties in this area are simply having a tantrum. It is essential to explore what the underlying causes might be. What might the learner communicating?
- Set the tone and share your own feelings. This might feel uncomfortable for some, but sharing our own feelings with our learners, modelling the responses and strategies that we use and encouraging them to do the same can have a really positive impact.

Chapter 9
FLEXIBLE THINKING

What is it?

Flexible thinking is the ability to consider a range of differing perspectives, adapting to changing situations and approaching problems from many different viewpoints. This skill allows learners to adjust their plans and ideas based on the latest information or unexpected circumstances. In perhaps its simplest form, it could be described as the mental flexibility to 'think outside the box' and not get fixed on one rigid way of doing something.

In our busy and changing world, it is important to be able to constantly re-evaluate the usefulness and effectiveness of what we know, what new information we have, what we are doing right now and what we should do next. We need to be able to make decisions, adapt and pivot quickly. This is especially important when we notice that something is not going to plan. Flexible thinking is crucial for dealing with uncertainty, solving problems effectively, adapting to changes and managing unexpected situations. It forms part of our resilience. The more flexible we are in our thinking, the more likely we are to bounce back and move on. It could be argued that flexible thinking is the skill that is the most necessary to get us through life!

> **REFLECTION POINT**
> * How is being a flexible thinker an asset to your current role in education?

Flexible thinking and classroom success

Have you ever taught a learner who ploughs on with a task even when they know that their approach is not harvesting success? It causes frustration for them as they constantly

DOI: 10.4324/9781003534075-9

experience failure and is difficult for us as teachers as, despite our best endeavours, nothing changes.

The ability to re-evaluate, problem solve, change direction and deal with uncertainty is the underpinning skill of being a resilient learner. Without the ability to think flexibly, our learners quite simply become stuck! If we can support our learners to be flexible thinkers, they will almost certainly learn more efficiently and effectively, as they will be able to think about things in many different ways. The following example illustrates how flexible thinking can be applied to pretty much any situation or problem to achieve classroom success:

Usman's pen has run out while was he working. If Usman is a flexible thinker, he may well think of multiple solutions to his problem, such as asking his teacher for a new pen, using his pencil as an alternative or borrowing a pen from a friend. If Usman is unable to demonstrate flexible thinking, he may think that there is nothing he can do about it, so he will not finish his work.

Thinking flexibly opens up our learners to many different opportunities, which helps them to learn and grow. It allows them to look at problems from different viewpoints and consider multiple ways to problem solve. Flexible thinking also helps learners to remain positive and have a growth mindset. Instead of getting upset and frustrated by problems, they can logically consider the different solutions that there may be.

When developing relationships in school, flexible thinkers are more likely to consider other people's ideas and take on board their opinions, which breeds valuable teamworking skills.

Flexible thinking can also help with the social aspects of wider school life. As flexible thinkers, our learners demonstrate a willingness to explore other people's opinions and take part in discussions, as opposed to believing that their opinion is the only correct answer.

REFLECTION POINT

- What challenges might a learner who is unable to think flexibly experience in the classroom?

Learners who find flexible thinking challenging may:

- have only one approach to a task which is used no matter how successful/unsuccessful it is;
- experience difficulties with recognising when an element of a task has been completed and it is time to move on;
- need support to transition from one task to another;
- have difficulties with accepting help from others;

- not demonstrate independent problem-solving skills;
- be perceived by others to be defiant;
- refuse to follow instructions and/or participate in activities;
- interpret things very literally;
- find it challenging to accept the viewpoints of others;
- prefer very regular routines; and
- follow routines and processes rigidly.

It is now time for another case study to being this to life: meet Jake.

Flexible thinking – a case study

Background information

Historically, Jake has always found thinking flexibly tricky. This has resulted in him experiencing friendship difficulties, as he has very set ideas about what games he will play with others and how they should be played. He experiences challenges in the classroom as he struggles with activities involving problem solving, debate and thinking from another perspective.

Jake does display strong leadership skills when the role involves directing others in a precise manner to get a job done. He excels at tasks where fact retrieval is particularly important to achieving success.

Information from the class teacher

Jake is brilliant at recalling facts related to the various topics we have studied in history, geography and science. He has incredible general knowledge. Jake finds tasks involving being creative, problem solving and thinking from the perspective of others much more challenging to access.

Often, group and partner work can pose problems as Jake finds it hard to accept direction from others or to take on board their ideas, wishes and feelings. This can lead him into conflict with his peers.

Observations
History: a debate about child labour in Victorian times

Jake had worked hard to prepare a list of reasons as to why he thought child labour in Victorian times was unacceptable. He demonstrated excellent recall of facts related to the Victorian era, showing sound knowledge and understanding of context. During the debate, Jake frequently became dysregulated when others disagreed with him. At points, he forcefully banged his fist on his desk. Often, he shouted over his peers as they presented their counterarguments. His teacher intervened several times to ask him to wait and listen to his peers. He did so but huffed loudly to communicate his annoyance.

PE: football

After practising various skills, including passing, dribbling and shooting, Jake and his classmates were put into teams to play mini games of football to allow them to apply their skills. When Jake's team played, he gave all members of his team clear directions as to where they should be and what their role was. Throughout the match, Jake shouted at his teammates if they did not do as he had told them and argued with the teacher, who was acting as the referee, if he disagreed with their decisions. Eventually, his teacher stopped the match and asked Jake to sit on the bench to calm down. He followed this instruction but loudly shared his opinion that: 'The match is stupid and the people on my team are stupid.'

Support and impact to date	
Support	Impact
Jake has participated in an intervention focusing on teamwork and team-building skills. This took place for 30 minutes per week for six weeks.	Jake did not complete the intervention, as he frequently disrupted the group by either being far too dominant and upsetting the group dynamic or choosing to opt out of the group because he wanted everyone to complete the tasks in the way that he felt was best. He did not respond to adult modelling or feedback.
Having a specific role within a group task which meant that he was not the 'leader'.	Jake was able to do his 'job' well, as he clearly understood what was expected of him in his role. However, he remained very publicly critical of his peers if they did not stick to their role or made an error.
Structured turn taking and attention tasks with a peer.	Jake took turns and enjoyed the various games and activities. He was able to wait and allowed the other child to have their turn. However, he does not always put these skills into practice in real-life independent play scenarios.

Next steps

Due to the increasing relationship difficulties that Jake is experiencing with his peers, it is time to look at reviewing his provision so that he can access classroom paired and group tasks, as this is becoming a more significant barrier to learning.

Flexible thinking toolkit

Classroom challenges

- Have only one approach to a task which is used no matter how successful/unsuccessful;
- Experience difficulties with recognising when an element of a task is completed and it is time to move on;
- Need support to transition from one task to another;
- Have difficulties with accepting help from others;
- Do not demonstrate independent problem-solving skills;
- Can be perceived by others to be defiant;
- Refuse to follow instructions and/or participate in activities;
- Can interpret things very literally;
- Find it challenging to accept the viewpoints of others;
- Prefer very regular routines; and
- Follow routines and processes rigidly.

Tools

1. Offer multiple choice answers to a question or solutions to a problem. Ask your learner to work through all of them, saying why each may be correct/incorrect. Draw their attention to the fact that they are exploring a range of perspectives and possibilities in completing this task.

2. Createopen-ended opportunities for your learner to suggest as many ideas and possibilities to answer a question or solve a problem as possible. They might like to brainstorm or mind-map their ideas. Encourage them to give as many responses as possible – no matter how unusual or unlikely.

3. Use puppets or small world resources to re-enact scenarios. Frequently pause to ask your learner to consider how each character in the roleplay is feeling and why that might be.

4. Model flexible thinking. Point out to your learner when you have changed your mind about something and why this is. This will give them a model to apply and show them that flexible thinking is part of everyday life.

5. Makesmall but noticeable tweaks to embedded routines and make the changes explicit to the learner.

6. Offer structured adult-led opportunities to engage in construction and crafting activities. When learners engage in this kind of activity often, they develop the ability to quickly shift focus from one thing to another, which builds their cognitive flexibility. Adding a peer to work with for this task also means that the learner will have to take on board another person's perspectives.

7. Play barrier games – activities where two or more people work together to complete a task but cannot see each other. Working with a barrier (eg, a large folder) between them, have one learner give instructions for the other learner to follow, then remove the barrier and compare results. Activities could include completing a map, making a tower of bricks in a particular colour order or describing a picture to draw.

8. Have your learner give two contrasting answers to the same question for debate. Provide them with a sentence starter to build upon - for example:

    Do you think chips should be banned from the school lunch menu?

    - Chips should be banned because...

    - Chips should not be banned because...

9. Explore 'What would you do if ...?' scenarios.

10. Use a visual timetable but add in an unexpected or surprise event. The learners are not to know what this is – for example:

Registration	Assembly	Writing	Snack time	Playtime	Geography	Surprise!

11. Play games but change the rules. For example, play Snakes and Ladders, but go up the snakes and down the ladders. Encourage your learner to make new rules or changes to games that they are familiar with.

12. Teach the meaning of idioms and figurative language in context – for example, 'You have green fingers' would best be taught in the context of the school garden.

13. For figurative language and idioms, look at the two possible meanings to work out what is really meant with accompanying visuals – for example:

> What could 'they get on like a house on fire' mean?
>
> or

14. Develop a structured problem-solving script to approach problem-solving activities. This could be made into a prompt card or lanyard for the learner to follow.

Images by Freepik

Here are five top tips to support learners in developing flexible thinking that you can share with a colleague:

	Flexible thinking – five top tips
	Model your own flexible thinking by describing out loud when you have changed your mind and why. This will show the learner that this is an everyday thing that we all do.
	When eliciting an answer from your learner, ask them to give more than one possibility to encourage them to consider alternatives.
	Ask multiple choice questions to force your learner to consider alternatives. Ask them to reason through why and why not each answer may or may not be correct.
	Plan surprise and unexpected events. Use a visual cue to prompt your learner that a surprise is coming. Talk about how they feel before, during and after the surprise.
	Encourage debate. Your learner could act as the debate moderator so that they can 'control' the scenario but not the opinions shared.

Images by Freepik

REFLECTION POINT

- What else would you consider of importance to share with a colleague regarding flexible thinking?

For parents and caregivers who may wish to learn more about supporting their child's flexible thinking skills, the following resource is something that you can share:

Flexible thinking – a quick guide

What is it?

Flexible thinking is the ability to consider a range of differing perspectives, adapting to changing situations and approaching problems from many different viewpoints. This skill allows learners to adjust their plans and ideas based on the latest information or unexpected circumstances. In perhaps its simplest form, it could be described as the mental flexibility to 'think outside the box' and not get fixed on one rigid way of doing something.

Children who find flexible thinking challenging might:

- have only one approach to a task which is used no matter how successful/unsuccessful;
- have difficulties with recognising when an element of a task is completed and it is time to move on;
- need support to transition from one task to another;
- have difficulties with accepting help from others;
- not demonstrate independent problem-solving skills;
- be perceived by others to be defiant;
- refuse to follow instructions and/or participate in activities;
- interpret things very literally;
- find it challenging to accept the viewpoint of others;
- prefer very regular routines; and
- follow routines and processes rigidly.

How can you support your child to develop their flexible thinking skills?

1. Model flexible thinking. Point out to your child when you have changed your mind about something and why this is. This will give them a model to apply and show them that flexible thinking is part of everyday life.
2. Make small but noticeable changes to embedded rules and routines at home.
3. Have fun with change by playing familiar games but changing the rules – for example, play Snakes and Ladders but go up the snakes and down the ladders.
4. Validate and acknowledge the emotions that your child experiences when managing change but establish clear expectations and strategies for dealing with them in a safe and healthy way.
5. Give advance warning of change and explain exactly what will be happening, when and why.

Images by Freepik

Here are three skill builder activities that you can try with your learner which focus on developing flexible thinking skills:

	Flexible thinking – skill builders
	The following activities are designed to help your learner to develop their task initiation skills. When completing these activities, it is important to draw specific attention to: • the skill that they are using; • why it works; and • how the skill can be transferred back to the classroom.

YES! **Yes, and...**	Play 'Yes, and …' This game will support your learner to accept and build on others' ideas. Start the conversation with a statement such as, 'It's a horrible day outside.' Have each learner add on a 'Yes, and …' statement – such as, 'Yes, and the clouds are grey' – until the story finishes.
Story switch-up	Tell a familiar story, such as Cinderella, but give it an alternative ending. To make it even more engaging and fun, you could draw a comic strip or having the learners use puppets to retell the story. Switching up something familiar boosts creativity.
A different use	Think of alternative uses for everyday objects. Ask your learner to think of different uses for various everyday items that they may have at home or in school – for example, a pen could be a microphone or a magic wand; a toilet paper roll could be a telescope; and a funnel could be a trumpet. This will develop creative thinking that is 'outside of the box'.

Images by Freepik

To close this chapter, let's go back to Jake to see whether anything has changed in Table 9.1.

TABLE 9.1 Jake's revised provision

Support	Impact	Suggested next step
Opportunities to explore both sides of a debate to consider more than one perspective. This was achieved by asking Jake to come up with two opposing arguments independently and then share them with an adult.	Jake found this difficult to begin with but has improved over time. He is now beginning to see that there is more than one way to look at something.	Jake is now ready to start sharing in debate activities with a peer. An adult will initially lead this and then withdraw.
Barrier games in which Jake has been the person that receives the instructions.	Initially, Jake found this very difficult as he wanted to take the lead. Over time, he has become more willing to take more of a back seat. Having a prompt card with the 'rules' for being a good partner in barrier games has helped. When needed, he is reminded to look back at these.	Support for Jake to transfer this skill to the classroom for group activities using his prompt card.
Playing familiar games but with new rules.	Jake has enjoyed this and has been willing to allow his peers to change the rules.	Continue with this but extend out to the playground.

CHAPTER TAKEAWAYS

- Flexible thinking is the ability to consider a range of differing perspectives, adapting to changing situations and approaching problems from many different viewpoints. This skill allows learners to adjust their plans and ideas based on the latest information or unexpected circumstances. In perhaps its simplest form, it could be described as the mental flexibility to 'think outside the box' and not get fixed on one rigid way of doing something.
- Children who find flexible thinking challenging might:
  - have only one approach to a task which is used no matter how successful/unsuccessful;
  - have difficulties with recognising when an element of a task is completed and it is time to move on;
  - need support to transition from one task to another;
  - have difficulties with accepting help from others;
  - not demonstrate independent problem-solving skills;
  - be perceived by others to be defiant;
  - refuse to follow instructions and/or participate in activities;
  - interpret things very literally;
  - find it challenging to accept the viewpoint of others;
  - prefer very regular routines; and
  - follow routines and processes rigidly.

FOOD FOR THOUGHT

As we bring our journey through executive functioning to a close, here are a few final things to consider:

- The different component parts of executive functioning are crucial skills that form not only a basis for classroom success but also a firm foundation for developing the necessary employability skills required for the future.
- They are essential for our learners to be able to access the National Curriculum and wider school life.
- Several simple tools can be utilised to support executive functioning as part of our high-quality adaptive teaching offer.
- What supports learners with executive functioning difficulties will be supportive for all.

I hope that somewhere in here, there will something that is of value to you and your learners so that they can develop the skills for lifelong success and the brightest tomorrow.

REFERENCES

Baddeley AD, Hitch G (1974). Working Memory. In Bower GH (ed) *Psychology of Learning and Motivation, Vol 2.* Academic Press, pp 47–89.

Bays PM, Catalao RF, Husain M (2009). The precision of visual working memory is set by allocation of a shared resource. *Journal of Vision*, 9(10): 7.1–711.

Cowan N (2001). The magical number 4 in short-term memory: A reconsideration of mental storage capacity. *The Behavioural and Brain Sciences*, 24(1): 87–185.

Gray, C. (1994) *Comic Strip Conversations: Illustrated Interactions with Students with Autism and Related Disorders*. Future Horizons.

Graziano, PA, Reavis, RD, Keane, SP, Calkins, SD (2007). The role of emotion regulation in children's early academic success. *Journal of School Psychology*, 45(1): 3–19. https://doi.org/10.1016/j.jsp.2006.09.002

Miller GA (1956). The magical number seven plus or minus two: Some limits on our capacity for processing information. *Psychological Review*, 63(2): 81–97. (Republished: Miller GA (1994). The magical number seven, plus or minus two: Some limits on our capacity for processing information. 1956. *Psychological Review*, 101(2): 343–352.)

Mischel, W, Ebbesen, EB (1970). Attention in delay of gratification. *Journal of Personality and Social Psychology*, 16(2), 329.

Shoda Y, Mischel W, Peake PK (1990). Predicting adolescent cognitive and self-regulatory competencies from preschool delay of gratification: Identifying diagnostic conditions. *Developmental Psychology*, 26, 978–986.

For Product Safety Concerns and Information please contact our EU
representative GPSR@taylorandfrancis.com
Taylor & Francis Verlag GmbH, Kaufingerstraße 24, 80331 München, Germany

www.ingramcontent.com/pod-product-compliance
Lightning Source LLC
Chambersburg PA
CBHW080844270326
41929CB00017B/2921